T0147444

The Camp Tripper

The Secrets of Successful Family Camping in Ontario

PATRICK DZIECIOL

iUniverse, Inc.
New York   Bloomington

The Camp Tripper
The Secrets of Successful Family Camping in Ontario

Copyright © 2010 Patrick Dzieciol

iUniverse books may be ordered through booksellers or by contacting:

iUniverse
1663 Liberty Drive
Bloomington, IN 47403
www.iuniverse.com
1-800-Authors (1-800-288-4677)

Because of the dynamic nature of the Internet, any Web addresses or links contained in this book may have changed since publication and may no longer be valid. The views expressed in this work are solely those of the author and do not necessarily reflect the views of the publisher, and the publisher hereby disclaims any responsibility for them.

ISBN: 978-1-4502-2625-7 (pbk)
ISBN: 978-1-4502-2627-1 (cloth)
ISBN: 978-1-4502-2626-4 (ebk)

Printed in the United States of America

iUniverse rev. date: 5/13/2010

Contents

Introduction

My most memorable days as a child were spent on family camping trips at Algonquin Provincial Park in Ontario, Canada. We would pile into my father's brand-new, copper-coloured 1966 Ford Fairlane 500 after school on Fridays and drive to the campground. When we were about halfway there, we would have sandwiches at a favorite picnic stop (which has long since been bulldozed to make space for a four-lane divided highway). After the sandwiches, we would continue driving for another two hours until we reached the campground. When we arrived, we were tired; however, we had to work feverishly to get the tent and dining shelter set up before nightfall. Once they were set up, we could breath a sigh of relief because we knew that we only had to blow up our air mattresses and lay out our sleeping bags before retiring for the evening.

The next morning, we would start the day off by exploring our surroundings and hiking along one of the park's many trails. Lunch would follow, after which we would usually head to the beach for a swim. In the evenings, we always had a campfire. My brother and I would toast marshmallows on our poking sticks. When the fire was out for the night, we would crawl into our sleeping bags to sleep under the stars.

Many of the tents back then were made of canvas, and we had a blue nine-by-nine-foot canvas tent with orange trim. My father designed our dining shelter, which was also made out of canvas, a couple of aluminum poles, ropes, and stakes. We would erect the two aluminum poles at each end of the picnic table. The poles would support the canvas over the picnic table, and the canvas would be tied down with the ropes and stakes. The dining shelter came in handy during rainy days when we wanted to stay dry. Although the Ford

Fairlane was spacious, my father maximized our cargo capacity by building a rooftop carrier so that we could pack a lot of our camping gear there and free up more space for a comfortable drive up north. Camping was huge in our family when I was growing up.

Camping has come a long way from those days. There is so much camping gear to choose from that beginners probably don't know what to buy. Back in the 1960s, we just took our chances and drove up to the campground without reservations. We were always able to get a campsite at our target campground. Campsite reservations can now be made by phone or through the Internet, and we usually never go camping during peak season without a reservation. Clothing has also evolved to the benefit of campers. Back in those days, I can remember that my footgear consisted of Dash running shoes and rubber boots. Now, there is so much footwear to choose from: running shoes, hiking shoes, hiking boots, walking shoes, training shoes, water shoes, sandals, Crocs, and boots. We also have various fabrics that can be worn over our bodies to accommodate the changing temperatures, precipitation, winds, and seasons, and now we are also able to "layer" our clothing to suit the changing weather.

Lake of Two Rivers, Algonquin Provincial Park

Although the camping gear and clothing have changed over the years, it is comforting to know that most of Ontario's beautiful provincial parks where I camped as a child are still very much the same. I still swim in the same lakes, hike on the same trails, and camp in the same campsites as I did when I was a child. Ontario is a paradise for camping and outdoor adventure, and this is what inspired me to write this book.

My wife Georgia and I have been taking our children camping every summer, since they were born. Jacob is twelve now, and went on his first camping trip when he was three months old. Aaron will be eight this year, and went on his first camping trip when he was nine months old. One of my goals is to take my children camping to as many campgrounds as possible in Ontario. We are struggling to achieve this goal because each year we end up returning to campgrounds that we enjoyed camping at in the past. I envy those of you who are just starting out camping with young families because I know how much I enjoyed going camping with my family over the years.

The Camp Tripper provides strategies for planning, leading, and participating in successful family car camping trips in Ontario. Through years of personal camping experience as a child, adult, and parent, with friends and on my own, I have discovered the secrets of how to enjoy all of my camping trips to the fullest. This book is for families who want to get introduced to car camping and for seasoned campers who want to integrate the experiences of others to improve their family camping trips. Collectively, these strategies can help you overcome obstacles and achieve family camping bliss! There are plenty of books on hiking, canoeing, cooking, and survival in the backcountry, but precious few on car camping, which is what the majority of campers do. To achieve a successful camping trip, you need to know how to research and select campgrounds, reserve campsites, purchase camping gear, estimate camping gear costs for your family, pack effectively, set up camp efficiently, create a trip agenda, prepare for various day trips, break camp, and maintain your camping gear. *The Camp Tripper* delivers tips to achieve this and provides helpful information on some campgrounds in Ontario.

My camping experience includes the following:

- Approximately five hundred nights of camping experience in tents, cabins, huts, yurts, and motorhomes
- Car camping, backcountry camping, canoeing, and hiking throughout Ontario
- Camping across Canada, the United States, and Europe
- Planning, leading, and participating in over a hundred camping trips with family and friends throughout the years

The purpose of this book is to provide you with the knowledge that you require to have successful and memorable family camping trips in Ontario. To make this book as useful as possible, I have organized it into chapters that follow the course of a camping trip from start to finish. The order of chapters is designed to ensure that you do not forget anything important when planning and going on your camping trips. Throughout the book, you will also find that there are various camping tips organized as follows: Camp Tripper Secrets (hints to enhance your camping trips) and What You Should Know (other tips about camping).

1 Trip Planning

Ontario has hundreds of great campgrounds that offer access to recreational opportunities, attractions, and beautiful natural environments. With all of the campgrounds in Ontario, it can be difficult to determine where to camp. How do you find campgrounds in the region of Ontario where you live? Should you camp at private or public campgrounds? How do you know what facilities and services are available at the campgrounds? This chapter will help explain how to research and select campgrounds that meet your needs when you are planning camping trips.

RESEARCHING CAMPGROUNDS

Campground brochures can be found in the chambers of commerce and tourist offices in villages, towns, and cities in your region. These brochures are usually free of charge. Ontario Travel Information offices provide the best hard copy collection of parks and campground information that I have found. You can pick up the Ontario Parks *Parks Guide* for the current year at Ontario Travel Information offices or at provincial parks campgrounds. This guide contains an overview of all campgrounds and day use parks in the Ontario Parks system. The guide showcases the parks by region with photos and information on fees, reservations, facilities, activities, rentals, and when the parks are open. You can also locate brochures for specific provincial parks, conservation areas, national parks, and private parks at the Ontario Travel Information and tourist offices. Your local library is another source of information.

Another good source for campground information is word of mouth.

There is nothing like listening to camping experiences that others have had. Oftentimes, campers can give you tips on the best natural features, activities, and campsites that particular campgrounds and parks have to offer. When I talk to others about their great camping trips, I make notes and add the campgrounds and parks to my wish list for future camping trips.

The Internet has undoubtedly become the best resource for researching campgrounds. From your home computer, you can research campgrounds, parks, events, and activities, and you can make campsite reservations anywhere in Ontario, as well as other parts of Canada, the United States, and the world.

In Ontario, the campgrounds are either public or private. Ontario's public campgrounds are split into national and provincial parks, as well as conservation areas that offer camping or day use facilities and services. The province of Ontario maintains the provincial parks and conservation areas, while the federal government maintains the national parks. Ontario also has hundreds of private campgrounds scattered across the province.

PUBLIC CAMPGROUNDS

Public campgrounds tend to not have as many facilities and services as private campgrounds. However, public campgrounds tend to be situated in larger, undeveloped environments that offer hills, lakes, rivers, beaches, forests, wildlife, and other natural features to explore. Activities include hiking, canoeing, kayaking, boating, fishing, biking, and swimming. When our family plans to engage in outdoor recreation, we usually stay at a public campground instead of a private one because we enjoy hiking, canoeing, biking, and swimming in a natural environment. For the most part, public campgrounds also tend to offer larger campsites with greater privacy.

Camping facilities are not offered at all parks in the Ontario Parks or national parks system. Some parks are day use with no overnight camping. Other parks are wilderness parks that are designed for backcountry hiking or canoeing, but with few facilities and services. You need to know what facilities and services are in place before reserving a campsite to ensure that you will not be disappointed. The cost of campsites can vary from park to park and is usually based on the amount of facilities and services, what the park has to offer, as well as the quality of the campsite. For example, you will pay more for campsites in campgrounds that offer the following:

- Electrical hookups
- Local water supply for drinking and cooking
- Flush toilets
- Showers

- Laundry
- Trailer sanitation station
- Better than average privacy, quality, size, location, or view
- Yurts, cabins, or other roofed accommodations
- Other facilities and services

PRIVATE CAMPGROUNDS

Private campgrounds are owned and operated by people instead of the government. Private campgrounds tend to be more commercially developed, providing more facilities and services than public campgrounds. Facilities and services include laundry, games, swimming pool, recreational facilities, transportation to attractions, electrical and water hookups, cable hookups, stores, restaurants, Internet, TV, movies, and so on, in addition to the facilities and services offered at public campgrounds. Private campgrounds tend to be well equipped with drive-through campsites that can easily accommodate large recreation vehicles (RVs). Private campgrounds are often situated near cities, towns, villages, and other desirable areas that tourists travel to.

We use private campgrounds when we want to camp near cities, towns, villages, or major attractions. Usually, you can arrive and set up camp quite easily, and everything you need is there. Kampgrounds of America (KOA) is a good example of a company that operates well-run private campgrounds, and there are about 450 KOA campgrounds across Canada and the United States. In 2009, we were visiting Quebec City for four nights. Rather than pay hundreds of dollars per night to stay at a hotel in Quebec City, we stayed at a nearby KOA campground for a fraction of the price. Jacob and Aaron loved it because there was a heated swimming pool, games room, jungle gym, and free Internet. As parents, we enjoyed it because it was located minutes from Quebec City and had everything that we needed. We made the reservation about one month in advance, over the Internet. From our experience, we have found that the fees that we pay at private campgrounds are about the same or slightly more than premium campsites in public campgrounds: around $35 per night.

INTERNET SEARCH FOR CAMPGROUNDS

The Internet is undoubtedly the best resource for researching campgrounds. The Internet can provide you with the following:

- Direct links to campgrounds and parks
- Up-to-date information on campgrounds, parks, facilities, services, activities, and current events

- Blogs that document camping experiences of other campers at various campgrounds
- Other places of interest in the region of your target campground

To research campgrounds and make campsite reservations on the Internet, enter a search engine in your Web browser, for example, www.google.ca. Once the search engine page appears, you can do searches for virtually any campground in any region. For Ontario Parks campgrounds, you can do a Google search on **Ontario Parks**, or type www.ontarioparks.com into your Web browser. The Ontario Parks Web site provides the information that you need for researching, planning, and reserving a campsite at any of Ontario's provincial parks.

The **Visiting Parks—Park Locator** menu (www.ontarioparks.com/english/locator.html) is accessible from the home page. This Web page allows you to locate parks alphabetically, on a map, close to home, or by facilities, services, or season. You can also search for operating parks, which have facilities and staff on site; for example, Algonquin Provincial Park. The Web pages display all of the activities and facilities that are offered at the park and allow you to access the **Reserve a Site** link: reservations.ontarioparks.com/en/

After you have selected a park from the Web page (reservations.ontarioparks.com/en/), you can do more research on the campsites. All Ontario Parks car camping sites are numbered, and you can get more information by moving your cursor over specific campsites and clicking on them. Just by moving the cursor over the campsite, you can see if the site has electrical hookups or not. Click on any campsite to get detailed campsite information, check availability, and make a reservation. Here are some links that will help you to quickly locate campsites at public and private campgrounds in Ontario:

PUBLIC CAMPGROUND LINKS—ONTARIO

National Parks—Research	www.pc.gc.ca/
National Parks—Reservations	www.pccamping.ca/
Ontario Parks—Research	www.ontarioparks.com/
Ontario Parks—Reservations	reservations.ontarioparks.com/en/
Ontario—Conservation Areas	www.ontarioconservationareas.ca/

PRIVATE CAMPGROUND LINKS—ONTARIO

Camping in Ontario	www.campgrounds.org/
	www.campingontario.ca/
	www.campontario.ca/
Kampgrounds of America	www.koa.com/

To do more extensive searches, you can refine the keywords that you enter in your Internet search engine. For example, entering a city, town, or region name plus "camping private" gives you the names of private campgrounds in that area.

SEARCH ENGINE MAPS

You can also locate parks and campgrounds through the Internet using a map tool, which is available through some of the search engines, e.g., Google Maps: maps.google.ca/maps?hl=en&tab=wl.

You can use this map as a starting point to scan all regions of Ontario for parks and campgrounds. The green areas on the map represent the larger national and provincial parks. Just press the map with the left button on your mouse and drag it. This will allow you to navigate all over the province. When you find an area that you wish to camp in, double-click it to zoom in on parks and towns on the map. Once park and town names are displayed, you can do other searches to learn more about the campgrounds in the area.

ONTARIO PARKS

According to the Ontario Parks *Parks Guide 2009*, there are 330 parks in the Ontario Parks system. This covers 9 percent of Ontario's land and water mass. The "Park Locator" menu on the Ontario Parks Web site displays these parks as "operating" or "non-operating" parks. There are over a hundred operating parks listed, and these are the parks where most car campers go because the parks have staff and facilities on site. Scroll through the list of operating parks and you will see that Ontario's most popular provincial parks are listed there. With so many parks in the Ontario Parks system, it can be a daunting task to figure out which park will be the most suitable for your camping trip. I've camped at more than thirty of the operating parks and found that they all have something special to offer. When selecting a park to camp at, our family first decides what activities we want to partake in. From there, we select a park that meets our needs. In other words, once we list the activities that we want to do when we go camping, selecting an Ontario Parks campground becomes much easier.

CAMP TRIPPER SECRETS: SELECTING ONTARIO PARKS CAMPGROUNDS

Beaches

Many of the best beaches in the Ontario Parks system are situated in provincial parks that are located along the Great Lakes. The best beaches that come to mind are in the following parks: The Pinery on Lake Huron, Killbear on Georgian Bay, Sandbanks on Lake Ontario, Long Point on Lake Erie, and Lake Superior Provincial Park on Lake Superior. Wasaga Beach has an excellent beach, but it is a day use park with no campground. You will need to camp at Craig Leith Provincial Park, which is about a half-hour drive away, and do day trips to Wasaga Beach. Sauble Beach on Lake Huron is another great beach; however, the closest provincial park is Sauble Falls, which is within walking distance. Other provincial parks along the Great Lakes that have great beaches include Inverhuron on Lake Huron, Port Burwell and Rondeau on Lake Erie, Presqu'ille on Lake Ontario, and Awenda on Georgian Bay. If you prefer camping on smaller lakes, there are great beaches in Arrowhead, Algonquin (Lake of Two Rivers) Balsam Lake, and Bon Echo Provincial Parks. There are many other great beaches in Ontario that I haven't had the privilege of swimming at yet.

Canoeing and Kayaking

Canoes and kayaks are available for rent at many of Ontario's provincial parks. The parks that offer the most lakes and rivers (and therefore the best canoeing and kayaking options) include Algonquin, Killarney, and French River. These parks also appeal to those who want to do overnight trips into the backcountry. Other parks that offer excellent opportunities for day trips include Grundy Lake, Arrowhead, Charleston Lake, and Silent Lake.

Cycling

Ontario Parks has some campgrounds with designated bike trails. Other campgrounds don't have bike trails; however, cycling is permitted on the campground roads. Many provincial parks also offer bicycles for rent. The parks that have great bike trails include Algonquin, MacGregor Point, Killbear, Rondeau, and The Pinery. Even without official bike trails, bicycles are helpful for exploring campground roads and getting around the parks quickly. Nowadays, many campers pack their own bicycles on their camping trips.

Groceries and Shopping

Most Ontario Parks have a grocery store within a few kilometres of the campgrounds that offer a limited selection of groceries, gas, camping supplies, and other merchandise. The bigger parks such as Algonquin and The Pinery have groceries, camping supplies, and other merchandise for sale within the park.

Hiking

All provincial parks that I have camped at offer hiking of some sort, whether it is on official trails, the beach, or campground roads. The largest parks tend to offer the most hiking trails and the longest hiking trails. Backcountry hikers will prefer parks such as Algonquin, Killarney, and Lake Superior. These parks also offer some of the best day hikes in the province. All of the other parks where I have camped also have great hiking trails for day trips. Arrowhead, Bon Echo, Charleston Lake, and Grundy Lake are among my favourite parks for day hikes.

Organized Activities for Children and Families

The Ontario Parks system is excellent for providing organized activities for children and families. Some activities include going on hikes, doing crafts, and attending talks and slide show presentations at the visitor centres and amphitheatres. The larger parks offer a bigger assortment of organized activities.

Picking Wild Berries

There are many provincial parks that offer opportunities for picking delicious wild raspberries and blueberries. The berries are more easily found in open areas such as meadows and along roadsides where there is lots of sunlight. Late July to mid-August is the time when the berries seem to be ripe for picking in the Canadian Shield country north of Toronto. Call the parks in advance and ask staff for more details.

Sports and Recreation

Some campgrounds have recreation fields for sports, which is appealing to those who want to toss a football, baseball, or Frisbee. Other parks offer playgrounds with jungle gyms for younger children to play on. I have found that many of the provincial parks along the Lake Erie shoreline have excellent playgrounds.

Wildlife Viewing

I have found that the best wildlife viewing is in the larger parks, which offer more space for the animals. I have seen more deer, moose, beaver, fox, birds, and so on in Algonquin and Killarney provincial parks than in any other parks where I have camped.

Length of Trip

Another way to decide on what parks to visit is to determine how much time you wish to spend there. Naturally, you will want to select parks that have enough to keep you occupied during your stay there.

Day Visits

Some parks are day use only, including Wasaga Beach, which offers a spectacular beach, and Petroglyphs, which offers the largest known collection of Aboriginal rock carvings in Canada. These parks do not offer camping and will appeal to those who just want to visit an Ontario Park for the day. There are other parks that have excellent day use facilities and camping. The French River visitor centre on Highway 69 is an excellent example. The centre has a museum and hiking trails, and it offers magnificent views of the French River. Algonquin Provincial Park offers an art gallery, visitor centre, logging exhibit, shopping, and restaurants. Bronte Creek has a small zoo, a playground, and a play barn for children.

Short Camping Trips (One to Three Nights)

If you are planning a short camping trip, consider some of the smaller campgrounds that Ontario Parks has to offer to avoid the crowds. Some of the smaller parks where I have enjoyed camping are Craig Leith, Green Water, Lake St. Peter, Port Burwell, and Rock Point.

Long Camping Trips (Four Nights or More)

If you are camping for four or more nights, you may prefer to camp at the medium to large-sized parks because they may offer more recreational opportunities and organized activities. The larger Ontario Parks campgrounds include Algonquin, The Pinery, Killbear, Sibbald Point, Sandbanks, Balsam Lake, Grundy Lake, Voyageur, Presqu'ille, Arrowhead, Earl Rowe, MacGregor Point, Awenda, Pancake Bay, Darlington, and Emily. Each of these parks have three hundred or more campsites for car camping. The above list is based on total number of car camping sites, not by geographical size of the park.

Please forgive me if I have not mentioned any of your favourite parks in the Ontario Parks system. Ontario is a large province, and there are many more parks that I haven't had the privilege of camping at yet. More details about specific hiking trails, bike trails, and canoe routes will be discussed throughout the book.

CONSERVATION AREAS IN ONTARIO

According to the Conservation Ontario Web site (www.ontarioconservationareas. ca/), there are about 250 conservation areas throughout Ontario that offer hiking, cycling, and skiing. Some conservation areas offer other recreational activities, including fishing, swimming, and rock climbing. Facilities include interpretive centres, museums, and other attractions. If you live in the Toronto area, there are many excellent conservation areas for hiking that are within a one-hour drive, including Spencer Gorge/Webster's Falls in the Hamilton Conservation Authority and Crawford Lake, Hilton Falls, and Mountsberg in the Halton Conservation Authority. Not all conservation areas in Ontario permit camping. The conservation areas listed above are for day use only. You can browse the Conservation Ontario Web site for conservation areas that permit camping.

NATIONAL PARKS IN ONTARIO

According to the Parks Canada Web site (www.pc.gc.ca/eng/index.aspx), Canada has forty-two national parks. Ontario only has five national parks: Bruce Peninsula, Georgian Bay Islands, Point Pelee, Pukaskwa, and the St. Lawrence Islands. Of the five parks, online reservations can only be made for Bruce Peninsula, which has spectacular hiking along the scenic sections of the Bruce Trail that traverses the park. The trail is not recommended for young children because it goes along cliffs and ridges as it follows the Georgian Bay shoreline. Georgian Bay Islands, Pukaskwa, and St. Lawrence Islands National Parks also offer camping. Point Pelee is a day use park.

2 Campsite Reservations

As the saying goes, "Failing to plan is the same as planning to fail," and this applies to getting a good campsite in a campground of your choice during high season! You should make reservations if you are planning an overnight stay at a popular campground in Ontario during July and August. Weekends are especially busy, including June and September, when the weather is warm. Long weekends during the summer are the absolute worst time to go camping without reservations. Although many campgrounds offer a portion of their campsites on a first-come, first-serve basis, it is inconvenient to line up at the campground office and wait for campers to vacate their campsites and hope that one becomes available to you. The campsites do not have to be vacated until checkout time, which is 2:00 PM at most parks. Then, you will have to wait your turn to get a campsite. If there is no campsite available, you will have to drive to another campground. I have done this a few times over the years, and it isn't a pleasurable experience to look for a campsite and set up camp in the dark, especially if you have hungry children in the backseat of your vehicle who are tired and cranky! We usually start researching campgrounds in January and make reservations as early as possible, in order to secure choice campsites for the year. For example, in Ontario's provincial parks, campsite reservations can be made up to five months in advance, and this is when we make our reservations.

WHAT YOU NEED

To use the Internet to make campsite reservations, you will need the following:

- To set up an online account on the campground Web site in order to make online reservations.
- Your arrival date, how many nights you will stay, how many people are in your party, and what camping equipment you will bring (tent, screen house, or RV).
- Web links to the campgrounds (see the previous chapter).
- A credit card to process the payment for the reservation.
- Other information, as requested (e.g., home mailing address).
- A computer printer so that you can print a copy of your reservation. Some online reservation systems will send an immediate e-mail confirmation to you with all of the details. If you are unable to get a printed or electronic copy of your reservation, then make sure that you record your campground, campsite number, arrival date, length of stay, and reservation number on a piece of paper.

RESERVING A CAMPSITE

The "Trip Planning" chapter discussed in detail how to select a campground to meet the needs of your family. Here are a few key points to remember when reserving a campsite through the Internet:

- **Campsites with hookups:** Campsites either have electrical hookups or they do not. Some campgrounds offer water hookups on the campsites as well. Private campgrounds tend to have more campsites with electrical and water hookups. Campsite prices will vary but will usually cost about $30 to $35 per night. Expect to pay about $5 to $8 more per night if the campsite has electrical hookups.
- **Cabins:** Some private campgrounds across Ontario are now offering cabins, which provide bunk beds, lighting, electrical power, and other extras. A basic cabin will cost about $60 or more. When booking a cabin, check to see if you will need to bring your own bedding (sheets, pillows, and blankets).
- **Yurts**: Yurts (spacious, roofed structures made out of canvas and wood framing) are becoming more popular at Ontario Parks campgrounds and are available for booking at select parks throughout the province. The cost is approximately $85 per night and includes beds, barbecue, propane, lighting, and heater. You will need to bring your own bedding.

What You Should Know: Rules and Regulations

Most campgrounds have rules and regulations for camping, which you should review before making a reservation. The rules and regulations are designed for the benefit and enjoyment of everyone at the campground and must be followed by all. Here are some of the more typical rules and regulations:

- **Alcoholic beverages**: If and where alcohol can be consumed.
- **Campfires:** If and where campfires are permitted.
- **Firewood**: Where you can and cannot obtain firewood.
- **Fishing**: Restrictions for live bait, excessive catch, or fishing without a license.
- **Forest**: Fines for cutting or removing trees and bushes from the forest.
- **Litter**: You may be fined for littering or not keeping a clean campsite.
- **Maximum days**: How long you can stay on a campsite.
- **Maximum people**: How many people are permitted per campsite.
- **Maximum vehicles**: How many vehicles are permitted per campsite and where extra vehicles must be parked.

Note: If you are planning on camping with two vehicles, then you will most likely be charged an additional fee for the second vehicle. The park staff may also ask you to park your second vehicle in a public parking area instead of in the campsite.

- **Noise**: Fines for excessive noise or foul language in the campground.
- **Shelter equipment permitted**: RV, tent, screen house, and tarps. Campgrounds usually specify what type of shelter equipment is permitted on each campsite. For example, you may only be able to erect one tent on small campsites, or the campground may not have campsites big enough to accommodate large RVs.
- **Speed limit**: Restrictions for driving in the campground.
- **Pets**: Whether pets are allowed in the campground and what the restrictions are.
- **Reservations**: If changes or cancellations are permitted.

Most campgrounds require that you provide your credit card so that they can process the payment and send you a reservation confirmation. For same-day reservations, you will still get a reservation confirmation.

CAMP TRIPPER SECRETS: RESERVING GREAT CAMPSITES

Consider these suggestions for reserving a great campsite that meets your needs:

- **Active children**: If you have children, select a campsite that is close to the playground, beach, or other recreation facilities.
- **Close to amenities**: Decide whether you prefer to be closer to the amenities, including flush toilets, shower stations, campground office, or store. Do *not* select campsites near these amenities if quiet time during the day and a good night's sleep are important to your family. You may have other campers trudging across your campsite to get to the amenities or be disturbed by the amount of noise from campers talking or opening and closing doors nearby.
- **Premium campsites**: Some campgrounds offer premium campsites that are considered to be better than average for size, location, quality, or privacy. We book premium sites whenever they are available. Premium campsites are usually about $5 to $6 more per night and are worth the money.
- **Quiet time**: If you value your quiet time, find out if the campground offers "radio-free campsites," meaning that radios and excessive noise are not permitted. If you cannot get a radio-free campsite, then select a campsite that is away from the main campground roads and other higher traffic areas, such as flush toilets, shower stations, campground office, or store.
- **Privacy**: Select a campsite that is on the perimeter of the campground or has ample space between campsites.
- **Reserve early**: This is the best way to ensure that you get the biggest selection of available campsites.

Remember to pack a copy of your campsite reservation to avoid any potential booking conflicts and errors when you arrive at the campground. If you are planning on going camping without a reservation, refer to the "Setting Up Camp" chapter for more on what to look for when selecting a great campsite when you arrive.

3 Car Camping Startup Costs

Camping gear can be purchased at camping, hiking, and department stores. Just walking through the aisles to see the camping gear and asking the staff questions about the equipment will quickly bring you up to speed on what equipment will be required for your camping trips. Camping gear changes year after year, and specific brands that are available now may no longer be available by the time you read this book. For this reason, this book does not include photos of all camping gear. You can research camping gear on the Internet, where you will see photos, product descriptions, costs, and warranties. The following stores have great Web sites for researching camping gear:

Canadian Tire	www.canadiantire.ca/AST/browse/5/SportsRec/Camping.jsp
MEC	www.mec.ca/Main/home.jsp?bmLocale=en&bmUID=12601 45672025
Wal-Mart	www.walmart.ca/
Sears	www.sears.ca/catalog/tents/1101739

Other stores that sell camping gear include The Bay, Zellers, and specialty camping, hiking, and outdoor stores.

This chapter lists camping gear you may wish to consider for your car camping trips. Please use these lists as a starting point when you determine what camping gear you need to purchase. You may already have some of the gear or choose not to acquire everything listed here for your camping trips. Also included are estimates of how much the camping gear costs at retail (in

2009), so that you can determine your approximate startup costs. The cost estimates were obtained by reviewing the above Web sites. Please note the following:

- **Cost estimates are listed for adults and children on a cumulative basis**: For example, if you have five people in your family, you need five sleeping bags. The cost is $100 per sleeping bag, which becomes a cumulative total of $500 for five sleeping bags. The cost of an axe is listed as $25 whether you have one or five people in your family. Why? You only need one axe for your family, so $25 is the cumulative total.
- **Cost estimates do not include sales taxes.**
- **Cost estimates are for mid-range, three-season (spring, summer, and fall) camping gear**: This covers the May-to-October time frame when most campgrounds are open.
- **Cost estimates assume that you are camping with a tent**: You need to ignore what is not applicable if you are camping with an RV or if you plan to rent roofed accommodations such as yurts or cabins instead.

The costs of canoes, kayaks, bicycles, fishing and backcountry equipment are not included here. Not everyone who goes car camping brings this equipment. Canoes, kayaks, and bicycles can also be rented at many campgrounds and will be discussed later in the book. We purchase mid-range quality camping gear for our family. We find that mid-range quality camping gear meets our needs. Consider these suggestions:

CAMP TRIPPER SECRETS: PURCHASING CAMPING GEAR

- **Make a list before you go shopping.**
- **Check around the house**: Before going shopping, check around the house to see if you already have equipment available that can be utilized for your camping trips.
- **Purchase at season's end to save money**: Tents, screen houses, and other camping equipment are priced to clear after July. If your camping trip is late in the summer or fall, you may want to hold off purchasing new camping gear until then. We saved $75 on a $250 five-person tent a few years ago

by purchasing it in the first week of August, when it was on sale. Make sure that you have the opportunity to use newly purchased gear immediately, so that you can exchange it if it is defective. Tents and screen houses often come with two-week in-store warranties, meaning that if something goes wrong, you only have two weeks to return it to the store.

- **Value**: You can usually find great quality and prices at army surplus stores. Department stores have the best prices, but not always the greatest value. Hiking, camping, and other outdoor stores have excellent quality camping gear and service; however, be prepared to pay more for better quality.

CAMPSITE GEAR

Campsite Gear	Cumulative Cost (in Canadian Dollars)				
	Adult 1	Adult 2	Child 1	Child 2	Child 3
Campsite aids: Hammock	$20	$20	$20	$20	$20
Campsite aids: Lawn chair	15	30	45	60	75
Campsite aids: Ropes	6	6	12	12	12
Campsite aids: Swiss Army knife or equivalent	25	50	50	50	50
Fire: Axe	25	25	25	25	25
Fire: Butane lighters (2) or waterproof matches	6	6	6	6	6
Fire: Folding saw	20	20	20	20	20
First aid kit	20	20	20	20	20
Life jackets	30	60	90	120	150
Light: Flashlights (LED)	20	40	60	80	100
Light: Lantern	35	35	35	35	35
Packing: Hockey bags	35	35	70	105	105
Recreation: Knapsack (daypack)	25	50	75	100	125
Shelter: Dining (screen house)	150	150	150	150	150
Shelter: Tarps	10	10	20	30	30
Shelter: Tent	100	150	200	250	250
Shelter: Tent repair kit	6	6	6	6	6
Sleep: Air mattress	30	60	90	120	150

Sleep: Air pump	7	7	7	7	7
Sleep: Foam pad (mat)	20	40	60	80	100
Sleep: Repair kit for self-inflating sleeping pads or air mattress	5	5	5	5	5
Sleep: Self-inflating sleeping pad (mat)	60	120	180	240	300
Sleep: Sleeping bag	100	200	300	400	500
Cumulative Cost	**$770**	**$1,145**	**$1,546**	**$1,941**	**$2,241**

Campsite Aids

Hammock: A hammock is great for spending leisure time reading at the campsite. Children can also use a hammock as a makeshift swing to play on with friends. The most important features to look for in a hammock are the frame (some are frameless), compactness (for easy packing), durability, weight, and use of fabrics that dry quickly when wet.

Lawn chairs: Lawn chairs are essential for comfort when having a campfire or just relaxing and reading or having a cup of coffee. Most campgrounds in Ontario provide picnic tables on campsites; however, picnic table benches are not comfortable when sitting for extended periods of time. The most important features to look for in lawn chairs are compactness (some are collapsible for easy packing), durability, weight, colours that hide stains, drink holders and fabrics that dry quickly when wet.

Lawn Chairs

Ropes: There are many needs for ropes on camping trips, and you should pack at least 100 to 200 feet. Ropes are required for hanging tarps over tents and dining areas, clotheslines, hammocks, and food packs from trees if camping in the backcountry. A twisted polypropylene (3/16th inch) rope is excellent because it has a low stretch factor, does not absorb water, and is abrasion resistant.

Swiss Army knife or equivalent: A Swiss Army knife is an essential tool to have on all camping trips. Multifunction knives are useful for cutting rope, opening bottles, and other tasks.

Fire

Axe: An axe is required for chopping wood to make fires. The butt end of the axe can also be used to hammer tent stakes into the ground when staking the tent or screen house. A compact axe with a twelve-inch handle should be sufficient for you. Larger axes require more skill, strength, and experience.

Axe

Butane lighters or waterproof matches: Plastic disposable liquid butane lighters are great because they are inexpensive, are reliable, and last a long time. A good practice is to pack two on every camping trip, in the event that one breaks or gets lost. Waterproof matches are also good; however, they are bulkier to pack, and over time the packaging tends to break down. Matches that aren't waterproof should not be used for camping because the matches will not light when damp or wet.

Folding saw: A saw is necessary for backcountry camping or car camping where precut wood is not readily available. If precut wood is available, a saw won't be necessary because the wood will already be cut to twelve-inch lengths for burning in the fire-pit. You still need to use an axe to split precut wood into smaller pieces for burning. When purchasing a saw, consider a folding saw because they can fold to save space and reduce the risk of injury while being carried.

First Aid Kit

A first aid kit should be packed on every camping trip for emergency purposes. It is especially handy on camping trips, because people can fall or get small cuts that need to be cleaned up and bandaged. The contents of the kit should be rechecked and replenished at least once annually. Here are some suggestions for what to include in the first aid kit: aspirin, Tylenol, antacid tablets, water purification tablets, antidiarrhea medicine, personal medication, bandages, antiseptic wipes, iodine, alcohol swabs, napkins, tape, scissors, sterile gauze, antibiotic cream, lip balm, burn ointment, and sunburn lotion. Most campgrounds are well stocked with first aid supplies as well.

Life Jackets

If you have life jackets, you should bring them on all camping trips, if plans include swimming, canoeing, or kayaking. Life jackets are especially useful for young children at the beach who are unable to swim well. Check the manufacturer's specifications on your life jackets annually, to ensure that your children have not outgrown them and that the jackets are not defective. Life jackets can also be rented at campgrounds that rent canoes and kayaks.

Life Jackets

Light

Flashlights: Once your children are old enough to operate them, they should have their own flashlights for trips to the washroom or walking around the campsite at night. LED flashlights are better because they provide many more hours of light. Pack extra batteries for the flashlights. Another option to consider is a crank flashlight. With these flashlights, a crank is turned to generate power for light instead of using batteries. Some of the crank flashlights come with other features, such as AM/FM radio or USB port, which can provide emergency power to a cell phone.

Lantern: Battery-powered lanterns are safe for use inside the tent and around children. If purchasing a battery-powered lantern, look for lanterns that can run six to nine hours when fully charged. Check if they are rechargeable from 120V AC outlets or 12V cigarette lighters in cars. If purchasing a non-rechargeable battery-powered lantern, check to see how many hours it will run without losing power. The less expensive ones use four D-cell batteries and lose power after a few hours. Propane-powered lanterns provide bright light and can run for many hours. Propane can be a fire hazard and should not be used inside tents.

Packing

Hockey bags: Hockey bags can be used to store and transport camping gear. The less expensive hockey bags can be purchased for about $35 per bag. The hockey bags also help to compress camping gear while in transit and keep gear clean and tidy when setting up camp. Another option is to use backpacks for packing camping gear. Once camp is set up, the backpacks can be used for day trips to the beach, on hikes, and so on.

Recreation

Knapsacks (daypacks): Knapsacks are essential for day trips, including hiking, canoeing, cycling, and fishing. Knapsacks that have separate pouches for water bottles on the outside are better because the water bottles are easily accessible. Consider purchasing knapsacks for children once they are big enough to carry them.

Shelter

Dining Shelter (Screen House)

A screen house provides shelter for dining and lounging. The top provides overhead shelter from the rain, and the screened walls keep the bugs out. Some screen houses have storm flaps that prevent rain from entering through the side screened walls. Screen houses come in various sizes, colours, and shapes.

Screen houses should be packed for all car camping trips to ensure that there is adequate coverage from rain, bugs, and wind. The weather in the Canadian Shield, just north of Toronto, can frequently change from hot and sunny to cool and rainy. In fact, it is not uncommon to go camping there for a week and have rain at least every other day. A screen house will minimize the impact of rain on any camping trip.

Screen House

If there is a lot of rainfall, you can easily get discouraged, pack up, and go home early from a camping trip. A screen house helps to mitigate the risks of bad weather and bugs. Instead of a screen house, some campers hang a tarp over their dining area while camping. This option provides protection from the rain and some wind protection but no bug protection. When purchasing a screen house, consider the following features:

- **Zippers**: Zippers may break if there is a lot of traffic going in and out of the screen house, especially with children. Screen houses with good quality zippers are worth paying extra for.
- **Storm flaps**: Storm flaps that drape over the screened walls are a must to help keep rain and wind out. This is essential when preparing and eating meals. The storm flaps help to keep you dry and prevent tableware from being scattered across the campsite from blowing winds.
- **Framing poles**: The framing poles should be durable, shock-corded, and designed to last a long time. Shock-corded poles are sequenced in sections and are held together by an elastic cord that runs through the insides and lengths of the poles for easy assembly. Avoid purchasing screen houses with bulky, heavy, hollow steel poles. These poles rust and buckle easily.

Many of the less expensive screen houses have these poles. Hollow steel poles can sometimes be repaired with car radiator hose clamps; however, this is only a temporary fix. Fiberglass poles are compact; however, they can crack and break over time, especially if they are not dried properly or are stored in a cold place where the temperatures can drop to below the freezing point. Duct tape can be used to temporarily repair cracked fiberglass poles; however, the poles will most likely need to be replaced. Aluminum poles are the best; however, they are very expensive.

- **Awning poles**: Awning poles allow the storm flap on the entrance to be propped up as a porch roof for the screen house.
- **Size:** The screen house must be large enough to house the picnic table that is provided at the campsite. Keep in mind that different parks have different sized picnic tables. Additional space is required for the cooler, dry food box, water container, dish and cutlery box, and other gear.
- **Waterproof**: There is no bigger nuisance than trying to enjoy supper while rain is dripping from the ceiling of the screen house. The screen house fabric should be waterproofed.
- **"Rip-stop" nylon**: If the screen house is made of nylon, little squares on the nylon indicate that it is made of rip-stop nylon, which is a good feature to have as it helps to stop the nylon from ripping and tearing. Nowadays, many of the less expensive screen houses are made of polyethylene, which is the tough, heavier material that tarps are made of. Although bulkier than nylon, polyethylene is quite waterproof.
- **Stakes**: Screen house stakes should be durable; otherwise, they may bend or break when being anchored. Aluminum or steel pegs will outlast the plastic ones.

Camp Tripper Secrets: Purchasing a Screen House

- **Size**: Twelve- by twelve-foot-square screen houses are ideal. This size ensures that your family will have sufficient space for the picnic table, people, and camping gear. If the picnic table is placed to one side of the screen house, there will be enough free space to relax and read in a lawn chair or store other camping gear. Many campers regret purchasing smaller screen houses; they struggle to get large picnic tables into them and are also challenged for space.

- **Storm flaps**: Screen houses with storm flaps are the best for all camping trips, as they provide additional coverage against rain, and wind.
- **Easy setup**: Some screen houses can be set up by one person, which allows for multitasking by your family when setting up camp.

Tarp

A tarp (tarpaulin) can be used as a canopy to provide overhead protection from the rain and can also be rigged to provide some protection from the wind. Less expensive tarps are made out of polyethylene, which is a lightweight, durable, waterproof material that can be purchased in various sizes. Tarps work great over picnic tables if not using a screen house. Many car campers also hang tarps over their tents to provide additional protection from the rain. A tarp should be considered mandatory for all camping trips, whether it is car, canoe, or backcountry camping. It can also be used as a makeshift shelter in the event that the tent breaks. In 2005, we were on a camping trip in Algonquin Provincial Park, when the main zipper broke on our tent door. We used a small spare tarp, measuring nine feet by twelve feet, to cover the exposed area while we slept. Luckily there was no rain and very few bugs that night. The same problem happened to us while camping at Arrowhead Provincial Park in 2009, and we used the same tarp a second time to keep the bugs and rain out while we slept. In both cases, we ended up driving to Huntsville the following day to purchase replacement tents. The following should help to determine what size of tarp(s) is appropriate:

Tarp Covering Broken Zipper on Tent

- **Tarp to hang over dining area:** It should be at least twelve feet by sixteen feet to provide coverage for the picnic table, dining gear, your family, and to be properly hung on a slant for drainage.
- **Tarp to hang over tent:** A tarp should be at least three feet longer and three feet wider than the tent that it is hanging over, to provide ample coverage from the rain. For example, a twelve- by sixteen-foot tarp is a good size to hang over a tent that measures nine by twelve feet.
- **Tarp for other uses:** Measure the length and width of what will be covered with the tarp and allow a little extra when purchasing the tarp. For example, a nine- by twelve-foot tarp is a good size for covering bikes during rainfall. There are many tarp sizes that range from six by eight feet to twenty by twenty-eight feet and larger.

Tarp Covering Bikes

Purchase at least 50 to 100 feet of rope for each tarp.

Tent

The purpose of the tent is to provide a place to sleep and shelter from the wind, rain and bugs. Tents come in various colours and shapes and sizes. For car camping, look for a single tent that is large enough to house your family. When selecting a tent, consider the following features:

Tent

- **Zippers, framing poles, rip-stop nylon, and stakes**: Review the notes that are listed under "Shelter: Screen House" in this chapter.
- **Waterproof**: The fly (the cover on top of the tent) provides protection from the rain; it should cover as much of the tent as possible to prevent water from leaking inside the tent. The better quality tents have a transparent waterproofing strip applied over the seams, which should help prevent leaks through the seams for years. If the seams have not been treated, you will have to seal the seams after purchasing the tent and on an ongoing basis to avoid water seeping into the tent. The "Maintenance of Your Camping Gear" chapter discusses how to waterproof tents. The "Setting Up Camp" chapter discusses hanging a tarp over the tent for an added layer of protection against rain.
- **Dry floor tub design**: With the dry floor tub design, the floor seams are elevated off the ground to help prevent water on the ground from seeping into the tent through the seams. The floor of the tent is stitched to the walls of the tent several inches off the ground. In the photo below, the floor seams can be seen where the blue and gray tent fabrics meet:

Tent—Dry Floor Tub

- **Vestibules**: Some tents have a vestibule attached at the entrance of the tent. The vestibule provides a sheltered storage area for shoes and some camping gear.
- **Easy setup**: Tents that can be set up by one person without assistance from a second individual are excellent.

CAMP TRIPPER SECRETS: PURCHASING A TENT

- **Size**: When sizing a tent for your family, the best strategy is to select a tent that is rated for one to two persons more than the size of your family to ensure that there is enough space in the tent. For example, if you have a family of four, you should select a tent that sleeps five to six people, so that there is a little extra space to move around in and store clothing bags. The extra space will also help prevent you from going nuts when confined to the tent because of unexpected rainfall.
- **Shape**: Square and rectangular tents provide the best use of space inside the tent.

- **Zippers and framing poles**: Based on my experience, it is usually the zipper or framing poles that break. It is worth paying more for a tent that has good quality zippers and framing poles.
- **Tent repair kit**: A small tent repair kit is useful for patching small tears and holes in the fabric of the tent. Tent repair kits usually have a piece of the nylon tent fabric, glue, and extra rope for staking the tent.

Sleep

A few years ago, our family went on a three-night camping trip to Balsam Lake Provincial Park, in the middle of May. The weather was unseasonably cold and wet for the entire trip. The temperatures dipped to 3ºC at night and there was constant rainfall. What I remember the most about the trip is that I was constantly shivering and unable to sleep more than one hour per night due to the cold and dampness. In fact, I got my best sleep by napping for an hour in the car in the afternoon.

I checked the temperature rating on my sleeping bag and found that it was rated to 5ºC. I thought that it was odd that I was so cold because the temperature fell only slightly below the rating on my sleeping bag, and I had an extra blanket to compensate for this. What's more, Jacob and Aaron slept effortlessly throughout the nights without shivering, and their sleeping bags were rated only marginally warmer than mine. Jacob and Aaron's sleeping bags were placed on top of foam sleeping pads in the tent. Foam pads insulate from the cold ground below, so this partially explained why they slept better than me. Thinking the nights wouldn't be very cold, I had packed an air mattress for use under my sleeping bag, for added comfort. This was a bad mistake because air mattresses do not insulate you from the cold ground.

I prefer to sleep on an air mattress because they are more comfortable than foam or self-inflating pads. The problem with air mattresses is that once inflated, there is virtually no insulation in them, just a thin layer of fabric and air. Even though Jacob and Aaron had sleeping bags that were rated only slightly better than mine, they were much warmer because they each had a foam pad under them, which helped to retain their body heat. Air mattresses only work well for summer camping when the nighttime temperature is warm. Air mattresses are not thick enough to provide insulation against a cold ground.

When I returned from the camping trip, I went to a few camping stores and did some research on sleeping bags to see if I could find out more about why I was cold in my sleeping bag. I wanted to see if my shivering in the cold and dampness was a by-product of my age or if there was some reason for the bag not keeping me warm. What I found was that sleeping bags can deteriorate over time, which diminishes their ability to keep you warm. This is due to normal wear and tear as well as excessive washing of the sleeping bag in washing machines. I also discovered that the temperature rating on the bag is subjective because everyone's tolerance to cold weather is different. The sleeping bags can be temperature rated by testing them with younger people who are more resilient and able to handle colder temperatures than me.

What I concluded from my cold camping experience was that I desperately needed a new sleeping bag and will only use an air mattress when the temperature does not get too cold at night. Seeing as I had been using my sleeping bag for about twenty-three years, I assumed that it had come to the end of its useful life. After using the bag for three additional weeks the following July in Europe, Georgia promptly donated it to less fortunate people at a campground in Frankfurt, Germany.

Since then, Georgia and I purchased goose down sleeping bags to replace our old hollofil synthetic bags. The goose down is rated to -7°C, which provides ample additional warmth from the cold for three-seasons camping in Ontario. I also found that down sleeping bags tend to outperform synthetic bags for warmth, durability, weight, compactness, and longevity. A good down bag will cost approximately twice as much as a good synthetic bag. I have tested the new sleeping bag on nights when the temperature has dipped to 0°C, and I am very happy with it because I am able to tolerate the colder weather more so now, even with my air mattress. We purchased less expensive synthetic bags for Jacob and Aaron, since they are rougher on their sleeping bags. The synthetic bags are rated to -5°C. The photo below displays the down (blue) and synthetic (red) sleeping bags.

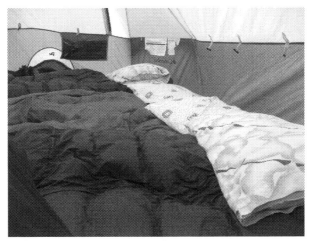

Sleeping Bags

Sleeping Bags

When selecting a sleeping bag, the following features should be considered:

- **Shell**: A nylon shell (exterior and interior) is the best for durability and to minimize drying time when wet. Most sleeping bags have nylon shells; however, some of the lower priced bags have other fabrics, such as cotton, for the inside shell. Liners can be purchased and inserted in sleeping bags for added comfort.
- **Fill**: Sleeping bags are filled with down, synthetic material, or a combination of down and synthetic material. Here is a quick overview:
- **Down filled**: Down (e.g., goose down)-filled sleeping bags are warmer than synthetic bags of equal weight. Down bags are also more durable and lighter, and can be compacted for storage more than synthetic bags. The main problems with down bags are they take a long time to dry and will not retain body heat well when wet. As long as down bags are kept dry, they are the better choice for car camping. Research seems to indicate that down bags last considerably longer than synthetic bags. Georgia and I paid $300 for two down bags at MEC in 2008.
- **Synthetic filled**: Synthetic (e.g., hollofil, polarguard, quallofil)-filled sleeping bags retain body heat when wet and also dry more quickly. Synthetic bags are also much less expensive than down bags. For backcountry camping, where there is a greater risk of the sleeping bag getting wet while canoeing and hiking, a synthetic-filled bag is the better choice, because it functions well when wet. We paid $160 for two synthetic bags at MEC in 2008 for Jacob and Aaron.
- **Temperature rating**: The price of the sleeping bag increases as the cold weather temperature rating of the sleeping bag decreases. Here is how the sleeping bags are generally rated in Ontario:

-15°C and colder	Winter sleeping bag
-15°C to +5°C	Three-season (spring, summer, fall) sleeping bag
+5°C and warmer	Summer sleeping bag

- **Bag shape**: The most common sleeping bag shapes are mummy and rectangular. There is also a barrel-shaped sleeping bag that can be found in some of the camping stores.
- **Mummy**: Most high-end sleeping bags are mummy shaped. These bags are tapered to the body to reduce cold air in the sleeping bag. As a result, the sleeping space is reduced and it is more difficult to move around during sleep. Because of the tapered design, mummy bags are smaller and can be compacted more than rectangular bags for storage. Mummy-shaped bags appeal to backcountry campers because of their lightweight and compact features.
- **Rectangular**: These bags are more spacious; however, it takes longer to warm up in a rectangular bag because there is more air inside the sleeping bag. If you move around a lot in your sleep, you will prefer the rectangular sleeping bag because it provides more space.
- **Barrel**: A cross between the mummy and the rectangular sleeping bags. They are not as tapered as the mummy bag and not as wide as the rectangular bag. Barrel bags are not as commonly available as mummy or rectangular bags. Some camping stores carry them.
- **Size:** Sleeping bags are generally available in short, medium, or long at camping stores. Department stores tend to not have as big of a selection in sizes. Pick a bag that is suited to your height.

CAMP TRIPPER SECRETS: PURCHASING A SLEEPING BAG

- **Temperature rating:** You should purchase sleeping bags that are temperature rated to handle the coldest nights expected on your camping trips. Check the average monthly nighttime temperatures of the region that you will be camping in. Your sleeping bags can always be unzipped on the warmer nights.
- **Best value:** A three-season rated, barrel-shaped bag that is down filled probably offers the best value for the money over the long term. A liner and blankets can easily be added for winter camping.

- **Purchase adult-sized sleeping bags for children**: Children will quickly outgrow child-sized sleeping bags. By purchasing adult-sized sleeping bags for children, you will get many more years of use out of the bags.

Sleeping Pads (Mats) and Air Mattresses

Most people cannot sleep well without a sleeping pad or air mattress under their sleeping bags. With just a sleeping bag on the floor of the tent, sticks, stones, roots, and other debris create a great deal of discomfort. The pad or air mattress will smooth out the ground below, so that you can sleep in comfort. We have air mattresses and sleeping pads (foam and self-inflating) and use them interchangeably to suit the type of camping trip that we go on.

Sleeping Pads, Air Mattress, and Foot Pump

Air Mattress

An air mattress must be inflated with a foot or power-assisted air pump. Self-inflating air mattresses are also available, but they are much more expensive. An upscale version of the air mattress is the larger "airbed," which is even more comfortable. Some of the airbeds are so large that they might not fit through the entranceway of the tent when inflated. Air mattresses tend to be bulkier and heavier than foam pads or self-inflating pads; however, air mattresses provide the most comfort for sleeping and are the best choice for car camping in the summer months. A few points to remember:

- **Good quality**: Good quality air mattresses are harder to find nowadays; they can be found for competitive prices at some army surplus stores. The plastic air mattresses should not be used, as they are not very durable.
- **Foot pump**: A foot pump can be purchased for about $7. Power-assisted (battery/electric) pumps are noisy and more expensive, and they cannot be used without a power supply at the campsite.
- **Repair kit**: A repair kit is recommended in case the air mattress gets punctured. Some air mattresses are sold with a repair kit. Over time, air mattresses can lose air along the seams and will need to be replaced.

Foam Pads

Foam pads do not require a pump and are light, durable, compression resistant, and waterproof. They insulate you from the cold ground below and can be punctured without impacting performance. Foam pads outlast the self-inflating pads and air mattresses and are less expensive. The only problem with foam pads is that they are the least comfortable for sleeping on. Foam pads are the best choice for cold and wet weather camping, due to their insulating and waterproofing features. Foam pads can be purchased in different lengths.

Self-Inflating Pad

Self-inflating pads fill with air when unraveled and the air valve is opened. Once inflated, you only need to blow into the valve a few times to achieve the ideal level of pressure before sealing the valve. Self-inflating pads insulate against the cold ground more than air mattresses, but less than foam pads. Self-inflating pads are much more expensive than foam pads and many air mattresses. As with air mattresses, self-inflating pads are usually sold with a repair kit. Self-inflating pads are more comfortable for sleeping on than foam pads, but not as comfortable as air mattresses. Self-inflating pads are suitable for car and backcountry camping.

CAMP TRIPPER SECRETS: SLEEPING PADS AND AIR MATTRESS

- **Achieve comfort while sleeping**: The number one goal of using sleeping pads or air mattresses is so that your family can sleep comfortably. If your family does not sleep well at night, they will not enjoy the camping trip and will want to cut the trip short and go home early. Sleeping pads or air mattresses should be packed on every camping trip.
- **Type of camping trip**: Air mattresses provide more comfort and are better suited to car camping in the summer. Foam pads and self-inflating pads are better suited to backcountry, wet, and cold-weather camping.
- **Best value**: A foam pad provides the best value because it is the least expensive, performs under any conditions, and will probably last the longest.

DINING GEAR

Dining Gear	Cumulative Cost (in Canadian Dollars)				
	Adult 1	Adult 2	Child 1	Child 2	Child 3
Cooking: 5- to 7-piece cookset	$25	$25	$35	$35	$35
Cooler: 16 quart (1 to 2 people) or 36 quart (3 to 5 people)	22	22	34	34	34
Tableware: Cutlery set (spoons, forks and knives)	15	15	15	15	15
Tableware: Dishes and bowls (unbreakable)	10	20	30	40	50
Tableware: Mugs (unbreakable and insulated) with lids	8	16	24	32	40
Tableware: Sharp cutting knives (1 to 2)	10	10	10	10	10
Tableware: Tablecloth (vinyl)	8	8	8	8	8
Tableware: Tumblers (unbreakable)	2	4	6	8	10
Storage: Plastic bins (2) for dining gear and dry and canned food	5	5	10	10	10

Storage: Plastic bottles	9	9	9	9	9
Stove: Fuel	12	12	12	12	12
Stove: Funnel	3	3	3	3	3
Stove: Single-burner or double-burner	45	45	85	85	85
Stove: Spare fuel canister	15	15	15	15	15
Stove: Toast rack	5	5	5	5	5
Utensils: Bottle opener	4	4	4	4	4
Utensils: Can opener	8	8	8	8	8
Utensils: Ladle	5	5	5	5	5
Utensils: Spatula	5	5	5	5	5
Washing basin	10	10	10	10	10
Water: Bottles for individual use	6	12	18	24	30
Water: Container for family use	10	10	10	10	10
Water: Filtration (pump)	70	70	70	70	70
Cumulative Cost	**$312**	**$338**	**$431**	**$457**	**$483**

Cookset

A five- to seven-piece cookset is suitable for family camping trips. We use a seven-piece set, which includes three pots with lids and a nonstick frying pan. Check around your home to see if old pots and pans can be given new life on camping trips.

Cooler

A thirty-six-quart cooler should be ample for three to five people. Some families pack an additional sixteen-quart cooler for drinks. When purchasing a cooler, check the temperature rating on the cooler to ensure that it would keep the ice solid for several days. Coolers with locking devices help to lock in cold air.

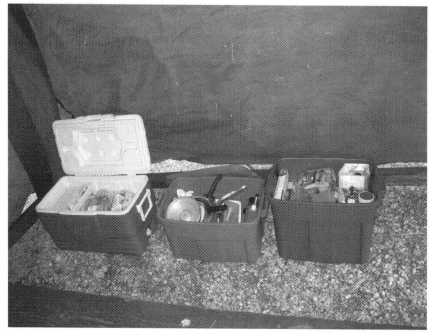

Cooler, Dining, and Dry Food Boxes

Tableware

- **Cutlery set:** A stainless steel set (spoons, knives, and forks) that is sized for your family.
- **Dishes and bowls:** A set of unbreakable dishes and bowls should be purchased for your family. Breakable dishes will chip and crack in no time and are dangerous around the campsite with children.
- **Mugs:** Mugs for beverages should be unbreakable, be insulated to maintain the correct temperature longer, and have lids. All adults and older children who will drink hot beverages should have mugs.
- **Knives:** Cutting knives should be sharp enough for cutting meat, and other knives should be large enough for scooping jam, peanut butter, or mayonnaise from the bottom of jars.
- **Tumblers:** An option for cold drinks.
- **Tablecloth:** A durable vinyl tablecloth works best on camping trips. These tablecloths can be wiped dry and are extremely durable.

Table Setup

Storage

Plastic bottles: Small plastic bottles with lids for pourable liquids and solids are handy for packing smaller quantities of spices, sauces, and vitamins, instead of packing the full-sized store bottles. Camping stores sell these bottles in sets of five to ten bottles of various sizes.

Plastic bins: Two large plastic bins with lids can be purchased for camping. One bin can be used to store all dining gear, while the other can be used as a "dry food" box. The dry food box would be used to store all food that does not go into the cooler. Plastic bins are durable, waterproof, and bug/animal resistant. Some campers prefer using cardboard boxes to store dry food; however, these boxes can easily fall apart, either through wear and tear or from moisture. Plastic bins can be purchased from large department stores and will last for years.

Stove

Some campers prefer to cook their meals on campfires, instead of on camping stoves. This practice is not recommended for several reasons. First, most people struggle with starting and maintaining a fire. What's more, it is very difficult to maintain the correct level of heat on a campfire to properly cook a meal without undercooking or burning it. In addition, firewood costs about $6 a bundle at most provincial park campgrounds in Ontario. You can quickly burn a hole in your wallet just trying to cook your meals over campfires. Finally, during dry weather conditions, many parks will impose fire bans and you will not be permitted to have campfires. A cooking stove is much more efficient and also saves on the environment because it slows down the depletion of dead wood and live trees in the forests. Here are some notes on camping stoves:

Stove and Supplies

- **Single- and double-burner stoves:** Most camping stoves have one or two burners; however, there are some with three burners. For family car camping, the double-burner stove, as shown in this photo, is perfect. A portable single-burner stove is a better choice for backcountry camping.
- **Liquid gas or propane powered:** Most camping stoves are liquid gas or propane powered. Propane-powered stoves require propane cylinders, and empty gas cylinders contribute to a growing garbage problem in our environment. Propane cylinders are considered to be hazardous waste and are not

accepted at landfill sites. Campgrounds have to hire firms that specialize in recycling leftover propane cylinders, and it costs money. Many campgrounds are now asking campers to take home their propane cylinders because it is a major problem to dispose of them. If you use a propane-powered stove, then please do not use disposable propane cylinders. Instead, use refillable propane cylinders or purchase a liquid gas camping stove. We camp with a double-burner liquid gas-powered stove.

- **Oven:** If you want to bake when camping, then you should purchase a stovetop or outback oven. The oven is mounted on top of your camping stove and can be purchased for around $70.
- **Liquid gas refillable fuel canister (spare):** If you have a liquid gas stove, you may want to consider purchasing a spare fuel canister, so that you have extra fuel for your stove.
- **Funnel:** If you have a liquid gas stove, you will need a small plastic funnel in order to pour the liquid gas into the fuel canister for the stove.
- **Toast rack:** A toast rack is a small metal rack that sits on top of the camping stove grill and is used to toast bread.

Utensils

Here are other utensils for the dish and cutlery box: bottle opener, can opener, ladle, and spatula.

Washing Basin

A plastic washing basin is required for washing cookware, dinnerware, and utensils. The washing basin can also be used for washing hands before meals. A good strategy is to purchase the largest washing basin that fits inside the dining gear bin.

Water

Bottles (individual use): Each person should have his or her own water bottle for drinking water. This is essential for day trips, around the campsite, and at the beach.

Container (family use): A large plastic container should be purchased for storing cooking, washing, and possibly drinking water. Large water containers are essential for reducing the amount of times that you will need to walk to the water station for refills. The water in most Ontario campgrounds is drinkable; however, you should check with campground staff before drinking it. Water containers can be purchased in a thick solid plastic shape, or in a thinner collapsible version that can be compressed for storage when not in use. I prefer the thinner collapsible version in order to maximize packing space in our vehicle.

Water Container, Point Farms Provincial Park

Water filtration (pump): If you intend to canoe or hike in the backcountry, consider purchasing a water filtration system, which is a pump that filters out bacteria to provide clean drinking water. The filter system is also useful in campgrounds that do not have safe drinking water. Another option is to purchase water purification tablets, which are sold at camping stores and many campgrounds. You can also boil water; however, this is time consuming and burns up a lot of stove fuel.

VEHICLE GEAR

Vehicle Gear	Cumulative Cost (in Canadian Dollars)				
	Adult 1	Adult 2	Child 1	Child 2	Child 3
Bike carrier	$140	$140	$140	$700	$700
Mobile 75W power inverter	30	30	30	30	30
Roof racks	200	200	200	200	200
Rooftop carrier (capsule)	250	250	250	250	250
Cumulative Cost	**$620**	**$620**	**$620**	**$1,480**	**$1,480**

Bike Carrier

If you are planning on taking bikes, you will need a bike carrier to mount on to your vehicle. The less expensive bike carriers mount on the back of the vehicle or on top of the roof racks. A rear mount bike carrier, which mounts to the back of the vehicle, can hold a maximum of three bikes and will sell for around $140. If you are transporting four bikes, a trailer hitch should be installed on your vehicle and a suitable bike rack can then be added to the trailer hitch. The trailer hitch with bike carrier will cost around $700.

Rear Mount Bike Carrier

Power Inverter

If camping at a campsite that does not have electrical hookups, consider purchasing a mobile 75W power inverter. This little device plugs into the cigarette lighter of your vehicle and converts 12V DC battery power to 120V household electrical power. This is brilliant because you can use this device to recharge batteries in cell phones, electric shavers, portable DVD players, and MP3 players.

Roof Racks and Rooftop Carrier (Capsule)

If you are challenged for space in your vehicle, consider mounting roof racks on your vehicle. You can fasten a rooftop carrier or capsule to the roof racks. The large rectangular capsules provide the most useable packing space for camping. If properly packed, the capsule should be able to hold at least 50 percent of your camping gear. This will free up space in your vehicle. Other campers use their roof racks to carry their canoes and kayaks on camping trips.

Roof Racks and Capsule

ELECTRICAL GEAR

Electrical Hookups at Campsite	Cumulative Cost (in Canadian Dollars)				
	Adult 1	Adult 2	Child 1	Child 2	Child 3
Appliances: Heater	$70	$70	$70	$70	$70
Appliances: Lamp	30	30	30	30	30
Extension cord (outdoor)	47	47	47	47	47
Cumulative Cost	**$147**	**$147**	**$147**	**$147**	**$147**

If you plan to select campsites with electrical hookups, consider the following:

Heater: A heater is great on the colder nights and allows you to extend your camping season when the weather is cooler. Before purchasing a heater, ensure that it is safe for camping and that it shuts off automatically when tipped over.

Lamp: A lamp allows you to read and play board games when it is dark. Select a lamp that is appropriate for outdoor use.

Other appliances: Some campers pack electric coolers on their camping trips. In the last four years, we have camped through at least five days of power outages due to storms at various campgrounds in Ontario. If you use an electric cooler, be prepared for power outages at campgrounds.

Extension cord (outdoor): Purchase a twenty-five-foot (or longer) outdoor RV extension cord, which is required to plug into the campground power supply.

Backcountry Gear

If you are planning on camping in the backcountry, you should refer to other books that focus on hiking and canoeing in the backcountry. Some of the gear listed in this book will be useful; however, there will be other gear that is specifically designed for backcountry camping that will be required. Some items that come to mind that are not covered in this book include backpacks, canoes, paddles, dry sacks, folding shovels, portable toilets, and smaller lightweight dome tents that are sized for one to three people.

Essential Gear for Beginners

The camping gear listed in this chapter is much more than what you really need to get started with family car camping. The following list suggests what camping gear is essential for beginners. If you are just starting out, consider borrowing what you can and only purchase what is absolutely necessary. Over time, as your camping experience grows, you can pick and choose what additional camping gear you need to make your trips more enjoyable.

Essential Camping Gear for Beginners	Cumulative Cost (in Canadian Dollars)				
	Adult 1	Adult 2	Child 1	Child 2	Child 3
Campsite aids: Ropes (100' to 200')	$6	$6	$12	$12	$12
Campsite aids: Swiss Army knife (or equivalent)	25	25	25	25	25
Cooler	22	22	34	34	34
Fire: Axe	25	25	25	25	25
Fire: Butane lighters (2)	6	6	6	6	6
First aid kit	20	20	20	20	20
Kitchen gear (borrow from the kitchen at home)	0	0	0	0	0
Light: Flashlight (LED)	20	40	40	40	40
Shelter: Tarp (for dining area)	10	10	20	20	20
Shelter: Tent	100	150	200	250	250
Sleep: Sleeping bags	100	200	300	400	500
Sleep: Sleeping pads	20	40	60	80	100
Stove (double burner for three or more people)	45	45	85	85	85

Water: Bottles	6	12	18	24	30
Water: Container (for drinking and cooking at campsite)	10	10	10	10	10
Collective Cost	**$415**	**$611**	**$855**	**$1,031**	**$1,157**

The total cost of your first camping trip will be the cost of the camping gear that is purchased, along with the cost of the camping supplies that are required for your camping trip. Camping supplies will be covered in the next chapter, "Packing for Camping Trips." Each successive camping trip will cost you less overall, because once all of your camping gear has been purchased, you only need to purchase supplies for your upcoming camping trips.

Looking to Skimp on Costs?

You can reduce your startup costs for camping by purchasing less expensive sleeping bags for approximately $50 each. Flashlights, tents, and other gear are also available for lower prices. But be forewarned; with lower prices come poorer quality and more aggravation and frustration when the equipment starts breaking down sooner than expected.

4 Packing for Camping Trips

This chapter discusses in detail what needs to be packed for family car camping trips. In addition to the gear discussed in the last chapter, you will need to pack clothing, personal needs, food, and other items.

Camping Gear

Use the lists in this chapter as a starting point when developing your own packing lists. Customize the lists by removing any items that you don't need and adding the items that you require. Notes are provided for items that were not listed in the last chapter.

CAMPSITE GEAR

	How Many Items to Pack				
Campsite Gear	*Family/ Adult 1	Adult 2	Child 1	Child 2	Child 3
Campsite aids: Clothespins	✓				
Campsite aids: Duct tape	✓				
Campsite aids: Dustpan and brush	✓				
Campsite aids: Hammock	✓				
Campsite aids: Lawn chair	✓	✓	✓	✓	✓
Campsite aids: Ropes (100' to 200')	✓				
Campsite aids: Swiss Army knife or equivalent	✓	✓			
Fire: Axe	✓				
Fire: Butane lighters (2) or waterproof matches	✓	✓			
Fire: Folding saw	✓				
First aid kit	✓				
Life jackets	✓	✓	✓	✓	✓
Light: Flashlights (LED) with spare batteries	✓	✓	✓	✓	✓
Light: Lantern	✓				
Packing: Hockey bags or large backpacks	✓	✓			
Recreation: Fishing equipment	✓				
Recreation: Knapsacks (daypacks)	✓	✓	✓	✓	✓
Recreation: Sports equipment and games	✓				
Shelter: Dining	✓				
Shelter: Tarps	✓	✓			
Shelter: Tent	✓				
Shelter: Tent repair kit	✓				

	Family/Adult 1				
Sleep: Air mattress, self-inflating pad, or foam pad	✓	✓	✓	✓	✓
Sleep: Air pump for air mattress	✓				
Sleep: Blankets	✓	✓	✓		
Sleep: Pillows	✓	✓	✓	✓	✓
Sleep: Repair kit (air mattress/self-inflating pad)	✓				
Sleep: Sleeping bag	✓	✓	✓	✓	✓

*Family/Adult 1 = Pack one set for the family or one item for Adult 1, whichever is applicable.

Campsite Aids

Clothespins: Pack at least ten clothespins to fasten wet socks, swimwear, and other small clothing articles onto the clothesline at the campsite.

Duct tape: Pack duct tape on every camping trip. It is essential for all kinds of repairs, many of which are documented throughout this book.

Dustpan and brush: A dustpan and brush are necessary to sweep out the tent and dust off the picnic table.

Recreation Equipment

Fishing equipment: If you plan to go fishing, you should call ahead to find out if fishing is permitted and what the rules and regulations are. Some provincial parks allow you to borrow a fishing rod and tackle for a day at no charge, so this may be another option to consider.

Sports equipment and games: Consider packing an extra hockey bag with sporting equipment, which includes baseball, baseball gloves, football, soccer ball, Frisbee, boogie board, mask, snorkel, fins, sand castle toys, and badminton set. Board games, cards, chess, checkers, and crossword puzzles are great to have when it is raining, as they help to pass the time away. Children can pack crayons and colouring books as well. Although these items will challenge the precious little packing space that you have in your vehicle, these items will provide enjoyment for your family and give your children more options with what to do with their free time.

Sleep

Blankets and pillows: Pillows are essential for getting a good night's sleep on camping trips. One to three old blankets should also be packed if cold nights are expected.

DINING GEAR

Cookset
Cooking: Tin foil
Cooler
Cooler: Ice block
Tableware: Cutlery set
Tableware: Dishes and bowls
Tableware: Mugs
Tableware: Sharp cutting knives
Tableware: Tumblers
Tableware: Vinyl tablecloth
Storage: 3 to 5 plastic containers
Storage: Elastic bands and twist ties
Storage: Plastic bags
Storage: Plastic bins (1 to 2) for dining gear and dry and canned food
Storage: Plastic bottles for pourable solids and liquids
Storage: Plastic wrap
Stove
Stove: Fuel
Stove: Fuel canister (spare)
Stove: Funnel
Stove: Toast rack
Utensils: Bottle opener
Utensils: Can opener
Utensils: Ladle
Utensils: Spatula
Washing: Basin
Washing: Liquid dish soap
Washing: Paper towels
Washing: Scrubbers
Washing: Washing cloth and drying towel
Water: Bottles
Water: Container
Water: Filter system pump

Tin foil: Tin foil can be used to wrap and bake potatoes in the fire-pit, or to place over a grill to cook meat.

Ice block: You should get in the habit of making your own ice block at home before each camping trip, since ice is required to keep the contents of your cooler cold. Several days before going camping, a large pot or plastic container should be filled with water, up to three inches from the top of the pot. The container can then be placed in the freezer and left there to freeze for several days. When packing for the camping trip, the container of frozen water should be placed upside down in the sink and hot water can be poured over it for a few seconds. When the ice block slides out, it can be double bagged and tied up. This ice block should last two to three days on the camping trip. Nowadays it is difficult to find ice blocks at campgrounds. Most campgrounds sell ice cubes, which melt more quickly.

Storage

Plastic containers: Three to five plastic (Tupperware-style) containers can be used for storing food and cutlery. Smaller plastic bottle containers can also be used for storing spices. I place my camera inside a large Tupperware container on every canoe trip. If the canoe tips over, the camera will survive in a waterproof floating container.

Elastic bands and twist ties: A handful of these items should be enough.

Large green plastic garbage bags: Five to ten large garbage bags are required for packing campsite garbage in. Most campgrounds have recycling in place; so organic garbage, recyclables, and other garbage need to be separated, as requested at the campground. Other uses for the green garbage bags include the following:

- Store firewood or camping gear inside garbage bags to keep it dry and tidy.
- Use bags as ground sheets for placing the cooler, dry food box, and dish and cutlery box on, to keep them clean from dirt.
- You can cut out slits in the garbage bag for the head and arms and use it as a makeshift raincoat.

Ziplock bags: Five to ten various sized ziplock bags are required for storing unpackaged foods inside the cooler, including cheeses, cold cuts, cut vegetables, and fruits. Ziplock bags are great for packing snacks for hikes, canoeing, and other day trips. Here are more suggestions:

- A large ziplock bag can be used to store bicycle repair parts and tools in.

- Items that can rust (including Swiss Army knives) can be stored inside ziplock bags until needed.
- Cameras and other electronic equipment can be kept dry in these bags.

Breathable fruit bags: Cherries and grapes are usually sold in plastic bags that have holes cut into them to make them breathable (many of these bags also have the ziplock feature). Wash out and save these bags whenever possible. These bags are excellent for packing and storing washed fruits and vegetables in the cooler on camping trips.

Plastic (cling) wrap: This can be used to seal in freshness on cut cheese, meat, vegetables, and fruit.

Washing

Dish washing cloth and drying towel: These are needed for washing and drying your cookware and tableware.

Liquid dish soap: Dish soap can be poured into a smaller plastic bottle, to save on space and to ensure that you only take as much as is needed for your camping trip.

Scrubber: This is useful for scrubbing pots and pans.

Paper towels: These are useful for wiping up and can also be used as napkins.

VEHICLE GEAR

Barf bucket

Booster cables

Candle and candle stand

Fill up tank, check fluid levels and tires

Fuses

Mobile 75W power inverter

Tools: 8" adjustable wrench

Tools: 8" pliers

Tools: Multibit screwdriver

Roof racks

Rooftop capsule

Vehicle maintenance and service

Most families probably find that they will log approximately 750 kilometres on an average car camping trip in southern Ontario. It is prudent to take some precautions to ensure that your family and vehicle are ready for the trip. Here are some considerations:

Barf bucket: An old plastic ice cream container can be packed under the back seat of the car. Why? To use as a barf bucket in emergency situations when someone gets carsick. Children can get carsick quite frequently on long car trips.

Booster cables: These can be used in case your vehicle battery dies and a boost is required from other campers.

Candle and candle stand: These can be used for warmth and light if there is vehicle trouble.

Fill up tank, check fluid levels and tires: Many campgrounds are in remote areas where there are no nearby service stations.

Fuses: A set of spare fuses should be kept in the glove box for emergencies.

Tools: Here are some tools that are useful to pack in the car: eight-inch adjustable wrench, eight-inch pliers (tongue and groove), and multibit screwdriver.

Vehicle maintenance and service: You should consider taking your vehicle in for maintenance and service just before the camping season starts for the year. This reduces the likelihood of vehicle problems during your camping trips.

ELECTRICAL HOOKUPS

Appliances: Heater
Appliances: Lamp
Appliances: Other
Extension cord (outdoor)

BACKCOUNTRY GEAR

As previously mentioned, if you are planning on camping in the backcountry, refer to other books that focus on hiking and canoeing in the backcountry.

CHILDREN'S GEAR

Baby food, bibs, formula, baby spoons, and soother
Carrying sack (baby carrier)
Diapers, wipes, powder, child potty, and change pad
Playpen
Stroller (collapsible), bug netting

The above list is directed at families with very young children.

Carrying sack (baby carrier): A carrying sack is used to carry very young children safely on a parent's back while hiking on trails. This gives parents much more mobility than a stroller, which restricts parents to campground roads. We used a carrying sack to carry Jacob and Aaron on short hiking trails (less than five kilometres), when they were under three years of age. The first photo shows an infant carrying sack, while the second photo shows a toddler (twelve to thirty-six months) carrying sack:

Infant Carrying Sack

Toddler Carrying Sack

Playpen: A playpen is extremely handy and gives you peace of mind when bringing very young children on camping trips. The playpen will also help prevent younger children from putting sand, stones, sticks, and other objects into their mouths.

Stroller (collapsible) and bug netting: A collapsible stroller is excellent for camping. Although you will be restricted to walking on flat smooth surfaces, it will do the job and will not take up a lot of storage space in the vehicle. Bug netting can also be thrown over the stroller and child for protection from bugs.

Stroller

BIKE GEAR

	How Many?				
Bikes	*Family/ Adult 1	Adult 2	Child 1	Child 2	Child 3
Bikes	✓	✓	✓	✓	✓
Bikes: Child carrier seat(s)	✓	✓			
Bikes: Helmets	✓	✓	✓	✓	✓
Bikes: Locks	✓	✓			

Bikes: Pant clips	✓	✓	✓	✓	✓
Bikes: Rack with basket and bungee cords	✓	✓			
Maintenance: Lubricate bikes before departing	✓	✓	✓	✓	✓
Maintenance: Tighten all bolts before departing	✓	✓	✓	✓	✓
Tools: Allan key set for bike	✓				
Tools: Bike air pump	✓				
Tools: Spare tire tubes	✓				
Tools: Tire repair kit	✓				
Vehicle: Bike carrier	✓				

*Family/Adult 1 = Pack one set for the family or one item for Adult 1, whichever is applicable.

Child carrier seat(s): Child carrier seats that mount on the back of bikes are great for carrying children between the ages of eighteen months and three to four years of age.

Child Carrier Seat, Lake of Two Rivers, Algonquin Provincial Park

Helmets, locks, and pant clips: Helmets are essential on biking trails, not only for your children, but for you as well. Bike locks should be considered if you plan on leaving bikes unattended at the campsite for extended periods of time.

Bike rack with basket and bungee cords: A basket mounted on top of the bike rack is an excellent choice for campers. A knapsack can easily be tossed into the basket and tied down with bungee cords for day trips. The basket is also useful for trips to the local grocery store when buying ice, milk, and other supplies. Finally, the basket is handy for storing helmets when camping, or while in transit to the campground.

Bike Rack with Basket

Maintenance: Bikes should be lubricated before each camping trip. The bikes may be exposed to rain, which can dry out and rust parts of the bike. All bolts should be tightened as well.

Tools for bikes: The following bike tools are useful on camping trips, in addition to the tools covered under "Vehicle Gear" in this chapter:

- **Allan key set.**
- **Bike air pump.**

- **Spare tire tubes.**
- **Tire repair kit**: This consists of patches, glue, and tools to remove the tire from the rim.

CLOTHING

One of the most discussed camping issues is how much clothing one should bring. Many hard-core backcountry campers only pack one change of clothes for their entire trip. Although this rule is practical for backcountry camping, families prefer a little more comfort on car camping trips. Most families prefer to pack no more than three days' worth of clothes, in addition to what they are wearing, for a seven- to nine-day camping trip. Most campgrounds have laundry facilities nowadays, and it is much easier to wash a few loads of clothes than pack a lot of extra clothes.

Another frequently discussed clothing question is what type of clothes one should pack for camping. For car camping, there is never really any immediate danger of suffering from changing weather conditions because help is always close by. One point to remember is to avoid cotton in cold wet weather. Cotton is very difficult to dry and loses its ability to keep you warm when wet. Acrylics keep you reasonably warm when wet, dry very quickly, and are not expensive.

Clothing	What to Pack				
	Adult 1	Adult 2	Child 1	Child 2	Child 3
Belt	✓	✓	✓	✓	✓
Clothing/gym bag	✓	✓	✓	✓	✓
Hats	✓	✓	✓	✓	✓
Jacket/coat	✓	✓	✓	✓	✓
Pants	✓	✓	✓	✓	✓
Pajamas	✓	✓	✓	✓	✓
Rain gear	✓	✓	✓	✓	✓
Shirts and undershirts	✓	✓	✓	✓	✓
Shoes	✓	✓	✓	✓	✓
Shorts and swimsuits	✓	✓	✓	✓	✓
Socks	✓	✓	✓	✓	✓
Sweater	✓	✓	✓	✓	✓
Underwear	✓	✓	✓	✓	✓

Towel	✓	✓	✓	✓	✓
Cold Weather Camping					
Boots	✓	✓	✓	✓	✓
Coat	✓	✓	✓	✓	✓
Gloves	✓	✓	✓	✓	✓
Snow pants	✓	✓	✓	✓	✓
Thermal underwear (top and bottom)	✓	✓	✓	✓	✓

Clothing/gym bag: You should consider using smaller bags for your clothing, as this will force you to cut down on how much clothing you pack for your trips.

Hats: Hats provide protection from the sun, rain, and bugs. Most people pack baseball hats; however, baseball hats do not provide the greatest protection from the sun. Hats with a brim offer better protection. Wool hats should be packed when camping in cold weather.

Jacket/coat: Jackets or shells that are water and wind repellant should be packed. An inexpensive shell will do. You should not listen to all of the hoopla about the more expensive waterproof shells. The more expensive waterproof shells provide protection from heavy rain; however, you will sweat like crazy in waterproof shells if using them for hiking, canoeing, or cycling.

Pants: You should avoid packing blue jeans on camping trips if cool, wet weather is expected. Jeans take a long time to dry and are very cold when worn wet. Just remember how long it takes to dry jeans in the dryer at home. Usually, the jeans are still damp when everything else is dry. You should look at other fabrics when packing for camping trips. If not sure what to pack, then just think of what dries the quickest in your dryer at home.

Rain gear: Waterproof shells for tops and bottoms provide the most protection from the rain. Some campers pack a poncho, which is a giant section of material that drapes over the body with slits for the head, arms, and legs. Ponchos can become awkward if you move around a lot, and rainwater will eventually drip onto your exposed arms and legs.

Two pairs of shoes: Each person should always have at least two pairs of shoes on every camping trip. If a shoe breaks, it may be difficult to find a shoe store near the campground. Secondly, if one pair of shoes gets drenched from water, it can take a few days to dry out the shoes properly. For summer camping, a pair of sandals or Crocs is great, with either hiking or running shoes. A good pair of hiking boots should be packed for any other time of year. Rubber boots are excellent for spring camping when the ground is soggy.

Extra shoelaces: Extra shoelaces come in handy if a shoelace wears through and severs on a camping trip.

Sweater: For cold weather camping, wool sweaters should always be packed. Many campers pack sweatshirts for summer camping instead. Sweatshirts are usually a 70/30 cotton/polyester blend. Again, because of the cotton, the sweatshirts can take some time to dry when wet; however, sweatshirts are much more comfortable than wool sweaters in the summer. It is a trade-off between practicality and comfort.

Thermal underwear: Thermal underwear should always be packed when camping during the spring, fall, or winter when the temperature is colder. Thermal underwear usually has a blend of fabrics, for example, 60 percent polypropylene, 32 percent wool, and 8 percent nylon. Because of the fabric blend, it won't itch against the skin and retains its ability to keep the person warm, even when wet. A wool sweater and Gortex shell can be added over the top, and wind- and water-repellant pants over the bottom, and you will be good to go under almost any three-season weather conditions.

PERSONAL NEEDS

Personal Needs	How Many?				
	*Family/ Adult 1	Adult 2	Child 1	Child 2	Child 3
Bathroom (personal hygiene) travel kit	✓	✓			
Binoculars	✓				
Books and magazines	✓				
Bug repellant	✓				
Camcorder (charged), battery charger	✓				
Camera and batteries	✓				
Car keys: 2 sets	✓				
Cell phone (charged) and battery charger	✓				
Compass or GPS (global positioning system)	✓				
DVD player (charged), battery charger and DVDs	✓				

	Family/Adult 1	Adult 2	Adult 3	Adult 4	Adult 5
Earplugs	✓				
Glasses: Reading, distance, sun glasses, contact lenses	✓	✓	✓	✓	✓
Health cards	✓	✓	✓	✓	✓
Laundry detergent or liquid	✓				
Maps	✓				
Medication, aspirin, Tums	✓				
Mirror (portable)	✓				
Mosquito coils	✓				
MP3 player (charged) and battery charger	✓				
Paper and pens	✓				
Phone numbers (work, home, other)	✓	✓			
Sewing kit	✓				
Sunscreen	✓				
Reservations	✓				
Trip medical and cancellation insurance	✓				
Umbrella/beach umbrella	✓				
Watch	✓	✓			
Wallet, all ID, credit and debit cards, and cash	✓	✓			

*Family/Adult 1 = Pack one set for the family or one item for Adult 1, whichever is applicable.

Bug repellant: The oily bug repellants last much longer and do a better job at keeping the bugs away than the "spray-on" bug repellants. Some people, especially children, prefer the spray-on repellants for comfort.

Compass or GPS (global positioning system): Nowadays many campers use a GPS, which is extremely accurate for navigation. If you are planning on traveling through the backcountry with a GPS, you should learn how to use it properly before going on your trip. The same applies if using a compass for backcountry navigation. A compass can be purchased for around $55, while a GPS costs more than $150. Whether using a GPS or compass, you should always have a map for backcountry travel to ensure that you are well prepared. I have never used a GPS or compass for backcountry trips and have always been able to rely on maps.

Earplugs: All light sleepers should consider packing earplugs when camping. There are all kinds of noises that can keep you up at night, including noisy neighbours, birds, rain, wind, vehicles passing by, and so on.

Laundry detergent: Laundry detergent can be packed when camping at campgrounds that have laundry facilities. If you are packing powdered detergent, you should consider packing it in ziplock bags. Estimate how many loads of laundry will be washed at the campground and have one ziplock bag filled with the correct amount of detergent for each load. If using liquid detergent, consider filling old vitamin bottles with the liquid.

Maps: You should always have maps for travel to the campground, backcountry, and surrounding region. This will ensure that you are adequately prepared for your trip.

Mirror: A portable mirror is required for personal hygiene at campgrounds that have limited facilities.

Phone numbers: Key telephone numbers that should be accessible on camping trips include work, auto club, auto mechanic, and family doctor.

Reservations: If campsite reservations have been made, present a copy of the reservation to campground staff to speed up the process of registering when arriving.

Trip medical and cancellation insurance: Cancellation insurance is normally only required if you will be booking costly camping trips where your family will be renting an RV or possibly flying to other locales to camp. Ensure that you have medical coverage, which protects your family, while you are camping in Ontario. If you reside in Ontario, then each member of your family should have an Ontario Health card. You will most likely need additional medical coverage if you are arriving in Ontario from other provinces, the USA and abroad for your camping trip.

Wallet, all ID, credit and debit cards, and cash: All citizens of the United States should carry valid passports when crossing the U.S. / Canada border for camping trips in Canada. The same applies for citizens of other countries. You will need to convert U.S. dollars, Euros and other currencies to Canadian dollars before heading off on your camping trips in Ontario. Most campgrounds in Ontario will not exchange money. Foreign currencies can be exchanged at banks throughout the province of Ontario.

MEALS

Breakfast

Bacon, sausages, eggs, toast, and jam

Cereal, fruit, and vitamins

Coffee, tea, and cream

Milk bags and plastic milk container

Pancake mix and syrup

Lunch

Bread, cheese, cold cuts, and peanut butter

Fruit and vegetables

Supper

Canned meats, pasta sauce, soups, stews, and vegetables

Dehydrated noodles, meats, rice, and soups

Hot dogs and buns, Kraft dinner

Meats: Sausages, chicken, steak, and hamburger

Fruit, vegetables, and potatoes

Condiments

Cooking oil or butter

Ketchup, mustard, relish, salad dressing, and other sauces

Salt, pepper, spice shakers, and sugar

Snacks

Candy, cereal, chocolate, and fruit bars

Chips, cookies, crackers, popcorn, pretzels, and trail mix

Juice boxes and pop

The meal items listed above work great for camping trips. You have the choice of cooking for hours to have the most exquisite meal in the campground or preparing quick meals that are less time consuming. We prefer to prepare quick meals that are nutritious and tasty. This way, everyone eats well, and there is more time to enjoy the camping trip. If the meal choices listed here are not appealing to you, then you should revise the list and bring what you like. You are restricted to stovetop cooking with camping stoves. Here are some points to consider when planning meals:

- **Pack the correct quantity**: Plan meals in advance to avoid over- or under-packing. Determine how many breakfasts, lunches, and dinners need to be provisioned for and pack accordingly. You can also consider packing a few extra meals, in case you decide to prolong your stay or have some friends drop by your campsite for a meal.
- **Lighten the load**: Canned meals contain a lot of liquid and are heavy. Dehydrated meals, including cereals, powdered soup mixes, rice, and noodles, are much lighter. After carrying the food box back and forth between the dining area and vehicle, you will quickly realize that less weight is best.
- **Pack frozen foods where possible**: Frozen meats and milk are great for camping trips. These items stay fresher when packed frozen and help to keep other items in the cooler cold longer.
- **Wash fruits and vegetables at home**: Fruits and vegetables should be washed at home and packed into the breathable fruit bags that were previously mentioned. This way, fruits and vegetables are ready to eat at the campsite. When packing fruits and vegetables in the cooler, priority should be given to the vegetables, since they spoil sooner.
- **Condiments, oils, and sauces**: The correct quantities of the following items should be packed in smaller plastic bottles, in order to reduce space and save waste: jam, pancake syrup, cooking oil, ketchup, mustard, relish, salad dressing, and other sauces. When the camping trip is over, the bottles can be washed out and saved for future trips. Plastic containers for pourable liquids and solids as previously mentioned can be used or old containers can be recycled. For example, plastic vitamin containers can be used to store jam, pancake syrup, and cooking oil.

CAMP TRIPPER SECRETS: PACKING EFFICIENTLY

- **Maintain a master packing list on your home computer**: If a master packing list is maintained on your computer, a fresh copy of the list can be printed for each camping trip. This will save you hours of frustration in writing a list for each trip. What's more, it can save you the aggravation of forgetting to list and pack something important, like a tent or sleeping bag. Over the years, your list should be updated to reflect your current needs.

- **Before going shopping**: You should check around the house for gear and supplies that you already have before going shopping, to avoid unnecessary expenditures. For example, you may have two spatulas in the kitchen; if the second one never gets used, add it to your camping gear to give it new life.

- **Compress gear before loading**: Tents, screen houses, and sleeping bags should always be packed in the bags and stuff sacks that they were purchased in to ensure that they are compressed when in transit. Pillows and other items can also be compressed, tied, and bagged to save space. Loose items can be packed in hockey bags, backpacks, knapsacks, and plastic storage bins to make them as compact as possible and allow for easy management at the campsite. Consider paying a little more for camping gear that is more compact, as this can save some frustration if you are challenged for space in your vehicle.

- **Drinking water**: You can call the campground before your arrival to see if campground drinking water is safe. Bringing cases of bottled water is a bad option because it takes up space in your vehicle and the empty bottles add to waste at campgrounds. Boiling water or using a water filter pump or water purification tablets are other options, as previously mentioned.

- **Buy groceries at home before going camping**: For the most part, the grocery stores near campgrounds will be more expensive and the selection is not as great as at home.

- **Camping with friends**: If camping with friends, you should determine who brings what, to avoid redundancy. For example, why pack two badminton sets when one set will do?

ESSENTIALS FOR BEGINNERS TO PACK

If you are just starting out camping and are still confused over what to pack, you may find this section helpful. To help clarify what to pack, this chapter and the "Car Camping Startup Costs" chapter can be reviewed in more detail. For the most part, common sense will dictate what to pack. You should allow plenty of time to plan, prepare a packing list, and pack for your trips.

Essentials to Pack for Beginners	**How Many Items to Pack?**				
	*Family/ Adult 1	Adult 2	Child 1	Child 2	Child 3
Campsite aids: Duct tape	✓				
Campsite aids: Dustpan and brush	✓				
Campsite aids: Ropes (100' to 200')	✓				
Campsite aids: Swiss Army knife (or equivalent)	✓				
Children's gear (see **Children's Gear** in this chapter)			✓	✓	✓
Clothing (see **Clothing** in this chapter)	✓	✓	✓	✓	✓
Cooler and ice	✓				
Dining gear (see **Dining Gear** in this chapter)	✓				
Fire: Axe	✓				
Fire: Butane lighters	✓	✓			
First aid kit	✓				
Light: Flashlights (LED)	✓	✓			
Meals (see **Meals** in this chapter)	✓	✓	✓	✓	✓
Personal needs (see **Personal Needs** in this chapter). Camping essentials include personal hygiene kit, bug repellant, sunscreen, health cards, and reservations	✓	✓	✓	✓	✓
Shelter: Tarp (for dining area)	✓				
Shelter: Tent	✓				
Sleep: Sleeping bags	✓	✓	✓	✓	✓
Sleep: Sleeping pads	✓	✓	✓	✓	✓
Stove and fuel	✓				
Washing basin	✓				
Water: Bottles	✓	✓	✓	✓	✓
Water: Container	✓				

*Family/Adult 1 = Pack one set for the family or one item for Adult 1, whichever is applicable.

ESTIMATING TRIP COSTS

Here is an easy way to estimate the costs of the camping trip. This example assumes that a family of four is going camping for one week. The first step is to add up the startup costs as in the "Car Camping Startup Costs" chapter. Along with startup costs, you need to add your trip costs and other costs as estimated below. The **Trip Costs** below are costs incurred on every camping trip. The **Other Costs** are examples of additional costs that will be incurred, if your family chooses to engage in those activities.

Estimated Camping Trip Costs for One Week: Family of Four

Startup Costs:	Your Estimate: See "Essential Gear for Beginners to Have" in last chapter	$
Trip Costs:		
Campsite reservations	$35/night for seven nights	$245
Gas	$60/tank, three full tanks	180
Groceries, ice, and stove fuel	Seven days	150
	Total Trip Costs	$575
Other Costs:		
Canoe rental, one day	One canoe, $40/day	$40
Bike rental, one day	Four bikes, $34/day (adult), $23/day (youth)	114
Entertainment	Take in local attractions, dinner, etc.	100
	Total Other Costs	$254
	Your Total Costs	$

Contrast camping costs with the costs of acquiring and maintaining a cottage or taking a trip to Disney World, and you can see that camping trips are very reasonable!

Packing for the Trip

5 Setting Up Camp

ARRIVAL

You should aim to arrive at the campsite as early as possible—at the very least, one to two hours before dark—in order to register at the office and set up camp. If your campsite is currently occupied, it must be vacated by the current occupants before you can set up camp, which is around 2:00 PM at most campgrounds in Ontario. Check your reservation to see when the campsite must be vacated by. This will enable you to plan to arrive at your campsite after the previous occupants have left. You should also avoid travel during Friday afternoon rush hour. This is the worst time for traffic when attempting to leave the city to go camping because others are leaving the city for their weekend trips as well. We try to book our campsites for arrival on Thursdays instead of Fridays. If we arrive on Fridays, we try to leave home Friday mornings so that we can beat the weekend traffic out of the city.

If your children are susceptible to carsickness, you may want to consider giving them a small meal, perhaps some dry crackers and soda, before the drive to the campground. Once you arrive at the campground, you need to stop and check in at the campground office. Present your reservation if you have one. After they have checked your reservation, they will ask you for your license plate number and the names of all the people in your group. They will then provide you with your campground permit (larger campgrounds may provide you with a map of the campground with all of the campsites marked on it). The permit is your confirmation of payment and registration. Some campgrounds provide two copies of the permit: one for your car and the other for inserting in a post on your campsite. Be sure to pick up a campground information guide or newsletter, if one is available. The information guide usually contains a campground map, campground rules, activities, and events, which will be discussed in more detail in the "Trip Agenda" chapter. At this point, you can claim your campsite and start setting up camp.

If you cannot get a reservation before leaving home, ensure that you arrive at the campground early in the day, as you will be given a campsite after all campers with reserved sites, and other campers without reservations who arrived before you, are given their sites. You can ask the campground staff to advise which campsites are available and then request to have a look at the campsites before selecting one. After selecting a campsite, you need to pay for it and get your permit before setting up camp. When selecting a campsite in person, consider these strategies for selecting great campsites:

CAMP TRIPPER SECRETS: SELECTING GREAT CAMPSITES

- **Safety**: If you have young children, avoid campsites that are along a ridge with a dangerous drop, close to slippery rocks, or close to deep water or busy roads.
- **Terrain**: A campsite should be flatter, with a higher spot for your tent, as opposed to campsites that are hilly or rocky, or have a basin that can potentially flood with rain.
- **Some sunlight**: This allows you to dry out any wet camping gear more quickly.
- **Avoid marshes and swamps**: Any campsites that are located near marshes, swamps, or other areas with stagnant water will have more than their fair share of mosquitoes. Avoid these campsites like the plague.
- **Arriving Friday night**: If you are arriving on a Friday night and plan to stay for two nights, pay for Saturday night as well to secure it. When arriving without a reservation, it is difficult to find campsites for Saturday night in the summer.
- **Ground cover**: If sleeping in a tent, grass under the tent provides added comfort and reduces wear and tear on the tent.

Refer back to the chapters on "Trip Planning" and "Campsite Reservations" for other strategies for selecting a great campsite.

What You Should Know:
Campsite Reservations

- **Don't Have a Campsite Reserved and All Campgrounds are Full?** Campsites usually pop up within one week before departure date, especially the last forty-eight hours, as other campers cancel their bookings due to unexpected circumstances. Have a few different campgrounds in mind, be flexible, and start calling up the campgrounds during the week before your target departure date to secure a campsite.

Good Campsite: Arrowhead Provincial Park

Camp Setup Strategy

Once you are at your campsite, it can take up to two hours to set up camp. You may choose to relax first, enjoy the surroundings, and set up camp later. Others prefer to immediately set up camp. We usually let the weather conditions and time of day that we arrive dictate when we will set up camp. For example, if you arrive in the early afternoon and the weather is great, then have lunch and go for a hike or a swim first. This ensures that you get at least one good day in, if the weather turns sour for the duration of your trip. If it is threatening to rain or getting dark when you arrive at your campsite, set up camp immediately to ensure that you are not scrambling around in the rain or dark. Here is our strategy for setting up camp when we are racing against time to set up camp before rain or dark:

Camping Gear

CAMP TRIPPER SECRETS: CAMP SETUP STRATEGY

1. **Know how to set up your camping gear**: If you have purchased a new tent or screen house, set it up at home before going camping. If you have purchased a new camp stove, practice starting it up, adjusting the heat level, and turning it off in your backyard before going camping. This will ensure that you have all working parts and that you know how to use your gear. Always pack the instructions for setting up and using your gear when you go camping, in case you need it.

2. **Tent**: Set up your tent first to ensure that you have a dry sheltered area for sleep. It is difficult and stressful to set up the tent in the dark or during rainfall. If it is raining when you arrive and the day is young, wait for the rain to stop before setting up your tent to ensure that your gear stays as dry as possible. If rain is expected until nightfall, then hang a tarp over the designated spot for the tent first (if there are trees to hang the tarp from). Once the tarp is up, you can spread out your gear and set up the tent under the tarp during rainfall, provided that there are no heavy winds.

3. **Dining area (screen house or tarp)**: Set up your screen house next to provide a sheltered area for dining and lounging. Move the campsite picnic table (if there is one) into the screen house to keep it dry, in the event of rainfall. If it is getting dark or starting to rain, move any camping gear that is dispersed across

the campsite into the screen house. If you are planning on using a tarp instead of a screen house, then set it up and move the picnic table and your camping gear under it.

4. **Hang a tarp over your tent:** This provides another layer of defense against rain and debris falling on your tent.

5. **Set up your beds:** Move your sleeping gear into the tent and set up the sleeping pads/air mattresses, sleeping bags, and pillows. If it is still daylight, consider deferring this step until later on in the day and move on to step six.

6. **Set up any other camping gear:** Set up a clothesline to dry towels, swimsuits, and other wet clothing. If you brought a hammock, then find a good spot to hang it. Any other camping gear, including lawn chairs and badminton nets, can then be set up. Move your cooler and dry food and dish and cutlery boxes into the dining area. This would also be a good time to set up the stove and prepare a hot meal.

7. **Plastic garbage bags:** Place one large plastic garbage bag in your tent. This will be your "dirty laundry bag." Whenever you need a change of clothes, toss the dirty clothes into the dirty laundry bag. Have a few other garbage bags set aside for regular garbage and recyclables. When the garbage bags are full, drop them off at the campground dump.

8. **Locate the amenities:** If you have not already done so, locate the nearest campground toilets, showers, and water supply tap. Ensure that you have asked the campground staff if the water is safe to drink, or if it must be boiled or treated first.

STEP-BY-STEP CAMP SETUP

Here are some step-by-step notes that will hopefully save you some frustration and agony when you set up your camp:

Tent Setup

Where to Place Your Tent on the Campsite

*   Select a spot that is higher and relatively flat with minimum stones, roots, and other debris.
*   A slight slope around your tent is good because rain can drain away from it.
*   Remove any sticks, stones, and other debris that could cause discomfort while you sleep.

- If there is a slight slope, position the tent so that your head is on the highest spot when you sleep.
- Do no put the tent on a low basin-shaped spot, as water collects there during heavy rain, and you may get flooded.

Flooded Area, Point Farms Provincial Park

- If you can position the tent between trees, it will be easier to set up a tarp over it. If you hang a tarp over your tent, do not anchor the tent with stakes or load your sleeping gear into it before hanging the tarp. This way you can reposition your tent to ensure that it is centred directly under your tarp.
- Ensure that the tent is away from the fire-pit and campground road for safety.
- Once you are satisfied with the positioning of the tent, shore up your tent with all of the stakes and guy-ropes provided.

The stakes and guy-ropes are provided for a reason: to stop your tent from blowing down. I remember one trip to James Bay where I set up my three-person dome tent carelessly and did not bother staking it down because I wanted to get on with exploring James Bay. The campground was on an island, and when I returned after several hours of touring, the tent had blown over, and I found it twenty-five metres away in someone else's campsite. Good thing that it didn't blow into James Bay; otherwise, I really would have been sleeping under the stars.

Tent Setup 1: Arrowhead Provincial Park

Tent Setup 2: Arrowhead Provincial Park

Tent Setup 3: Arrowhead Provincial Park

Tent Setup 4: Arrowhead Provincial Park

Tent Setup 5: Arrowhead Provincial Park

Tent Setup 6: Arrowhead Provincial Park

Ground Sheet

A ground sheet can be used to reduce cold and dampness that rises from the bottom of the tent. If you use a ground sheet, place it inside the tent, on top of the tent floor. This way, any rain falling on the outside of the tent will drain into the ground and you will have an extra layer of protection beneath you, inside of your tent. You can fold the ends of the ground sheet up along the inside walls of the tent to protect sleeping bags and pillows from rain that may seep in through the tent walls. I can always spot the new campers at campgrounds because many of them place a ground sheet or tarp under their tent with the edges of the tarp protruding out from the perimeter of the tent. When this is done, the campers will surely get soaked from the underside because the rainwater running down the side of the tent will collect on the tarp under their tent; it cannot drain into the ground and will therefore seep into their tent.

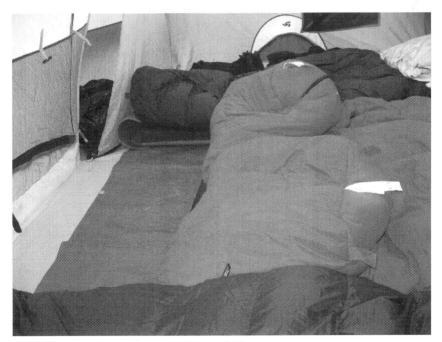

Ground Sheet

Have the Following Handy When Setting Up Your Tent, Screen House, and Tarps

- **Axe:** Hammer the stakes into the ground with the back end of the axe.

- **Spare stakes and guy-ropes:** Stakes and guy-ropes can easily break or get lost.
- **Duct tape:** For small repairs to framing poles, tent fly, tent, screen house, and tarps. If a framing pole breaks, you can wrap duct tape around the broken section; this may help to keep the pole operational until you can replace it or get a new tent. Likewise, the duct tape can repair small holes in the tent, screen house, and tarps. Duct tape has allowed me to continue several camping trips with broken framing poles.

Dining Area Setup

Where to Place Your Screen House on the Camp Site

- Follow the applicable strategies listed in the "Tent Setup" section above. The screen house should be placed on the second-best spot on the campsite (place the tent on the best spot).
- Once the screen house is set up, move the campsite picnic table (if there is one) inside the screen house. Level it by placing stones or wood chips under the legs of the picnic table where needed.
- Consider placing the picnic table off centre, inside the screen house, to allow for more usable space.

Screen House Setup1: Arrowhead Provincial Park

Screen House Setup 2: Arrowhead Provincial Park

Screen House Setup 3: Arrowhead Provincial Park

Screen House Setup 4: Arrowhead Provincial Park

Screen House Setup 5: Arrowhead Provincial Park

Screen House Setup 6: Arrowhead Provincial Park

Ground Cover

- Screen houses do not have floors in them, as they are designed to cover picnic tables and chairs and would rip if they had flooring built in.
- As mentioned in the "Packing for Camping Trips" chapter, place green garbage bags on the designated spots inside your screen house for your cooler, food box, dish box, and anything else that you constantly take in and out of the car. This will minimize the amount of dirt that gets tracked into your vehicle and also keep your camping gear clean. We pack extra green garbage bags for this.

Tarp Setup

If you do not have a screen house, you should hang a tarp over your dining area. If you plan to "wing it" without one, you are asking for trouble. Having a poorly sheltered dining area is probably one of the biggest reasons why camping trips end early.

Consider hanging a tarp over your tent as well. Most tents will eventually leak with heavy rain, and the tarp provides the first layer of defense by deflecting most of the rain away from the tent. Having a drenched tent and sleeping gear is another reason why camping trips end early. A few years ago, we were on a nine-day car camping trip in Algonquin Provincial Park, when it rained almost every day. The inside of our tent was dry, with only a little dampness on the bottom of the air mattresses (we forgot to pack a ground sheet to keep the moisture away from the air mattresses). If the tarp is hung properly over the tent and overhangs the tent by at least two to three feet on all sides, it will keep most of the rain away from the tent. The tarp also protects the tent by reducing the amount of falling branches, sap, and other debris that hits the tent. You will also find that with the rain hitting the tarp first, it muffles the noise of the rain while you sleep. In all our years of hanging tarps over our tents, we have never been drenched inside the tent during heavy rainfall. This photo demonstrates how you can hang a tarp using surrounding trees:

Tarp Hung Over Tent: Mew Lake, Algonquin Provincial Park

How to Hang Tarps

- Unravel the tarp and position the tarp between trees, so that you can tie the ends of the tarp to the trees.
- If there are only two trees to work with:

- Feed the rope through the grommets (hoops/holes) on one side of the tarp.
- Tie one end of the rope to one tree, as high as you can.
- Tie the other end of the rope to the other tree, again, as high as you can.
- At this point, two corners (or one side) of the tarp should be hanging between two trees.
- The other two corners of the tarp can be staked to the ground with ropes and tent stakes, if there are no other trees available.
- This will create a "lean-to"-style shelter.
- If there are four trees to work with:
- Ensure that the tarp is higher on one side than the other to allow for proper water drainage.
- Ensure that there are no dips on top of the tarp where water can pool. The tarp needs to be reasonably tight, so that all water drains off. If too much water accumulates on top, it will rip the tarp loose from the ropes. This has happened to me on a few occasions.
- Once the tarp is hung, you can adjust the corner ropes to get the proper height and tension. Ensure that the tarp is high enough to avoid contact with your head and any flames from your stove.
- If the tarp flutters too much, then tie off some of the grommets on the sides of the tarp to other trees or to stakes in the ground. This also takes some stress off the corners of the tarp and provides better rigging for high winds and rain.
- Rainwater will drain off the lower end of your tarp, so ensure that it is not pooling where your tent is; otherwise, you may end up with a swimming pool under your tent.
- To allow for better ventilation when hanging a tarp over a tent or screen house, hang the tarp high enough so that it doesn't make contact with the tent or screen house.
- Over the course of your camping trip, the ropes can slip down the side of the tree trunks due to winds. This will lower your tarp. To prevent the ropes from sliding down the side of the trees, tie the rope just above a tree branch whenever possible.
- Four trees are ideal because you can tie ropes from each corner of the tarp to a different tree. It is important to feed the ropes through the grommets along the sides of the tarp. If you only tie down the tarp to the corner grommets (as in the previous photo, "Tarp Hung Over Tent"), a high wind can easily rip the

grommets out of the tarp, and your tarp will be ready for the trash heap. This happened to me recently when I didn't take the time to set up the tarp properly.

- If trees are not available on your campsite, the alternative approach is to drape the tarp over the tent and stake it down, as depicted in the next photo:

Tarp Draped Over Tent: Grundy Lake Provincial Park

Bed Setup

- If using a ground sheet inside your tent, ensure that you have placed it on the tent floor first.
- Your sleeping pads or air mattresses will need to be unraveled, inflated, and placed in the tent.
- If there is a slight incline where the tent is placed, position the pads and air mattresses so that your head rests on the highest spot. Never sleep with your head by the entrance of the tent, as others can accidentally step on you while moving in and out of the tent at night.
- Remove the sleeping bags from their stuff sacks, unravel them, ruffle them up a bit, and then lay them over the pads or air mattresses.
- Add pillows and blankets if you have them.
- Have a flashlight handy in the tent.

Hammock Setup

- You need two sturdy trees that can hold the weight of you and your hammock.
- Ideally, the trees should be nine to twelve feet apart and away from the fire-pit and road for safety.
- Tie equal amounts of rope between the hammock and tree trunk on each end.
- The ropes should be fastened to the tree trunks about five to six feet above the ground.
- It is good practice to tie the ropes just above where the branches meet the tree trunk to prevent the ropes from slipping down the tree trunk.
- The hammock should be high enough so that when the heaviest person in your family lies in the hammock, he or she does not scrape against the ground. The hammock should also be low enough so the shortest person in your family can climb into the hammock.

Hammock: Lake of Two Rivers, Algonquin Provincial Park

Clothesline Setup

- You need two sturdy trees that can hold the weight of your clothes, towels, and sleeping bags.
- Ideally, the trees should be more than ten feet apart and along the perimeter of the campsite to ensure that members of your party do not accidentally walk into the clothesline.
- Hang the clothesline to the tree trunks, just above where the branches meet the trunks, to prevent the clothesline from slipping down the trunks.
- Hang the clothesline at least six feet high to ensure that people do not accidentally walk into it.
- The clothesline should be as tight as possible because it will flex with the weight of your clothes, towels, and sleeping bags.

Clothesline: Arrowhead Provincial Park

Tying Knots

You should have a basic understanding of how to tie some knots. Otherwise, you will struggle with hanging your tarps, hammock and clothesline. Although there are many books on ropemanship, all that you need to do is look up "quick release knot," "two half hitches," "power cinch knot" or just "knots" on the Internet and you will find that there are many Web sites that provide you with illustrations. Do a few screen prints of the knots and practice them until you gain the confidence to tie the knots properly. You do not need to know how to tie a lot of knots to set up camp. Believe me, I am one of those campers that only knows a few knots.

With a little wind and rain, you will find that some of your knots can become impossible to undo and you will resort to cutting them with a knife. My advice: learn to use the quick release knot and use it as much as you can. This will allow you to undo knots quickly, rather than having to cut ropes with a knife in frustration, when it is time to break camp.

YURTS

A yurt is a very spacious, roofed structure made out of canvas and wood framing. It can accommodate six people, due to its sixteen-foot by sixteen-foot octagonal shape. The yurt is well suited for strong winds, rain, and snow. In 2009, we rented a yurt in Mew Lake, Algonquin Provincial Park. We had heavy rain and were able to stay dry and warm because the yurt was elevated off the ground, was sufficiently waterproofed, and had a heater. We cooked all of our meals on the barbecue, which also had a hot plate. The barbecue was situated outside of the yurt, in a sheltered lean-to structure that provided protection from precipitation.

The yurts in Mew Lake have two sets of bunk beds, a table, chairs, electric heat, lighting, electrical outlet, barbecue with propane, cookset, and utensils. You will not need to pack your tent, air mattresses, sleeping pads, and a large portion of your cooking gear. Just throw your sleeping bags and pillows on top of the bunk beds, which have futon-style mattresses, and you will be ready to go. Pack your screen house so you have a sheltered area for the picnic table when you arrive. The yurt that we booked cost us about $85 a night, with taxes included.

Yurts are available for rent in some of Ontario's largest and most popular provincial parks, including Algonquin, Bon Echo, Bronte Creek, Killarney, MacGregor Point, Pancake Bay, The Pinery, Quetico, and Silent Lake.

Yurt: Mew Lake, Algonquin Provincial Park

Inside Yurt

WHAT YOU SHOULD KNOW: YURTS

- **Payment**: You need to provide a deposit on your credit card when you arrive, as insurance against any damage to the yurt or to cover the cost of missing contents. The deposit is returned after the yurt inspection upon your departure.
- **Key**: The yurt has a lock on the door; you will be provided with a key after registering. They key must be returned to the office by checkout time on departure day, and all of your personal contents must be removed by that time as well.
- **Yurt inspection**: Before your departure, staff will inspect the yurt and charge you for any damage or missing contents. It is your responsibility to clean out the yurt and remove all personal contents before the inspection. The "leave no trace" rule applies with yurts. If you don't clean out the yurt, Ontario Parks staff will clean it and bill you for it. Once you return the key to the office, staff will inspect the yurt within a half hour.
- **Cookware**: With our yurt, cookware had to be requested and rented separately for an additional fee.
- **No pets**: Pets are usually not allowed inside the yurt or on the yurt campsite.

- **Yurt furniture**: Furniture cannot be removed from the yurt.
- **No food or combustible fuels can be stored inside yurt.**
- **No smoking, cooking, or any open flame inside yurt.**

You can find out more at the www.ontarioparks.com Web site.

CABINS

Cabins are available for rent at many private campgrounds, including the KOA chain, which has over 450 campgrounds across the United States and Canada. Last summer, we rented a cabin at the KOA campground near Quebec City. The cabin was great because it could accommodate four people and was very reasonably priced. Most cabins are made of wood and are at least twelve feet by twelve feet. KOA campgrounds tend to be situated very close to major cities and desirable towns and villages.

The KOA cabin that we rented had two sets of bunk beds, a desk, chair, electric heat, lighting, electrical outlet, and old-style barbecue that required wood or coal. There was also a cold water supply on the campsite, outside of the cabin. We did not need to pack our tent, air mattresses, or sleeping pads; however, we needed our cooking gear. The campsite had a picnic table; however, the campsite was too small to set up a screen house on. The cabin did, however, have a porch, which provided ample space to eat on. The cabin that we rented cost us about $60 a night, with taxes included, which was a fraction of the price that the hotels in Quebec City were charging. When making reservations, check with the campground to determine if they supply bedding or cooking gear, so that you know what you need to pack.

We enjoyed our camping experience in a cabin at a private campground. As it was a cool and wet summer, we were able to stay dry and warm because the cabin had a heater and sat on an elevated wooden platform, above ground level. The cabin was totally waterproof and windproof, as it was well built. There were many extras included at the KOA campground: heated swimming pool, whirlpool, jungle gym, games room, free Internet access, billiards table, giant indoor chess game, store, restaurant, and so on. There was no running water inside the cabin; however, the public toilet, shower, and laundry facilities were easily accessible and very clean. In addition, the staff was very knowledgeable and was able to help us plan our tours of Quebec City. When booking a reservation, we were charged the first night's accommodation as a deposit, and the balance was payable at the end of our trip. The cancellation policy is also very good, because they will return your deposit less a $10 administration fee. For the most part, your responsibilities are similar to those that you have when you rent a yurt at a provincial park. Read the documentation at the campground to ensure that you abide by the rules.

RECREATION VEHICLES

RV camping is very popular across Ontario. Many years ago, we rented a class C motorhome in Toronto and drove it through Ontario, Quebec, and the United States, as far south as the Great Smokey Mountains National Park in Tennessee. We stayed at campgrounds that were equipped for RVs throughout that trip and had a great time. A few years ago, we rented another class C motorhome in Germany and used it to drive through Germany, France, Switzerland, Austria, and Italy. Class C motorhomes are built with the cab on a cutaway chassis, are gas or diesel powered, and are usually less than thirty feet in length.

Other RVs that you can drive include class A and B motorhomes, truck campers, and converted vans. RVs that are towed include the entry-level "fold-down" "pop-up," or "tent trailers." From here, you can upgrade to the larger travel trailers and fifth wheels. RVs can be equipped with everything that you need for a luxurious camping trip, including beds, dining table, fridge, stove, sink, cupboards, heating, air conditioning, shower, sink, toilet, TV, and stereo.

Class C Motorhome

Campsite Considerations for RVs

If you want to utilize all of the facilities with your RV, you need to select a campsite that meets the following requirements:

- It is large enough to house your RV.
- It is designed so that you can easily back in or tow your RV through it.

- It has electrical hookups so that you can utilize the appliances that require electricity.
- It has water hookups if you plan to use the sink, toilet, or shower.
- It is reasonably close to a sewage dumping station, so that you can empty out your sewage tanks.
- It has reasonably level ground, so that you can easily level the RV with your levelers.

Most Web sites, including the ones listed in the first chapter of this book, allow you to easily determine which campsites will be suitable to campers with RVs and trailers.

6 Trip Agenda

After arriving at your campground, always check the brochures and park information guides that are available at the campground office. Not only will the office have a good collection of hard copy information for the area, but staff can also advise you of upcoming events at the campground and surrounding area. This will help you to build an agenda of activities for your camping trip. Ontario Parks campgrounds also have a park information guide, which resembles a newspaper and highlights the activities and events taking place at that particular park.

Park Information Guide

The park information guides that are available at Ontario Parks campgrounds are generally your best overall source of information for planning your car camping trip agenda. These guides usually have information on the following:

- **Events**: organized hikes, children's activities, and educational programs
- **Backcountry camping:** the latest information on local conditions
- **Campfires**: where to obtain wood, campfire bans, and campfire regulations
- **Campground**: maps, location of facilities (showers, toilets, and tap water), rules, and regulations
- **Environment**: forests, rivers, lakes, and other environmental features and concerns

- **Garbage**: disposal and recycling programs
- **Park amenities**: stores, visitor centres, and exhibits
- **Recreation**: hiking trails, biking trails, canoeing, swimming, and fishing
- **Rentals and outfitters**: canoes, kayaks, small boats, and bikes
- **Tips**: safety, wildlife viewing, and avoiding wildlife encounters
- **Other information**: local weather radio channel, emergency local contacts, trailer and RV dumping stations, and advertisements from local businesses, including restaurants, shops, gas stations, vehicle and RV repair, camping equipment, and other accommodations

If the guide is available at your campground, you should use it as a cornerstone in planning your camping trip agenda because these guides have everything that you need to get your trip going,

BUILDING YOUR TRIP AGENDA

When building your camping trip agenda, you will find that most activities can be categorized as follows:

- Beach and swimming
- Campfires
- Canoeing, kayaking, and boating
- Cycling
- Exploring the region surrounding the park
- Fishing
- Groceries and shopping
- Hiking
- Organized activities for children and families
- Picking wild berries
- Sports and recreation (badminton, baseball, football, Frisbee, etc.)
- Walking around the campground roads and walkways
- Wildlife viewing

When we go camping, we build agendas for camping trips that can be up to nine days long. Our family gets together to discuss the activities, and we collectively decide what we will do. In order to have a successful camping trip, everyone's input should be considered. By adding some structure to your trip, you will ensure that you get to do some, if not all, of your desired activities. We try not to do too much per day, to ensure that we do not get exhausted.

For example, if we go on a four-hour hike, we will not go on a canoe trip on the same day. We find that three to four hours on one activity constitutes a major part of the day, and the rest of the day should be spent on shorter activities or just some R&R around the campsite.

Here are some very important considerations for your day trips:

- **Plan activities based on your experience level**: Always look at the canoeing, kayaking, cycling, hiking, and swimming abilities of everyone in your family and plan the activities based on the abilities of the least experienced person. This will ensure that everyone gets enjoyment out of the activity.
- **Common sense**: Start your canoeing, kayaking, cycling, or hiking trips first thing in the morning to ensure that you are back before the end of day. Plan to complete your trip at least two hours before dark to ensure that you have a few hours to spare if you fall behind schedule. Make a mental note of what time you leave, so that you can monitor your progress and more easily estimate your return time.
- **Free days**: Build in extra time or "free days" where you just "wing it" and do things spontaneously. Sometimes, the free days end up being the best days on your camping trip.
- **Weather forecast**: The best way to organize the agenda is to do it by weather. Listen to the local weather forecast and plan your agenda accordingly. You do not want to have your beach day on a cold or rainy day.

SAMPLE TRIP AGENDA

Here is a sample agenda for a camping trip that is nine days long. More details follow in this chapter:

Day One: Arrival
- Pick up a park information guide or campground brochure when you arrive at the office. Ask the staff at the office what activities are available if there is no guide or brochure.
- If you arrive early and the current occupants have not left the campsite, you can use that time to have lunch at the beach or picnic area, drive or walk around the campground and get familiar with the campground and facilities, or do a short hike.
- Once you have claimed your campsite, set up camp.

- Purchase some firewood before dark so that you are able to enjoy a fire on your first night.
- Pick up any groceries that you forgot to bring from home.
- Check the local weather forecast to determine what weather conditions you will have for the next few days. You should get an updated weather forecast daily, in case you have to make changes to your trip agenda to suit the weather.
- Discuss the activities available with your family and plan your trip agenda day by day.

Day Two: Hiking

- Select a trail to hike, prepare for it, and do the hike. If the trails are short, you can do a second trail.

Day Three: Canoe Trip

- Refer to the information guide or brochures to determine what canoeing options are available.
- If you plan to rent, get more information on where to rent the canoe and rent one for a day trip. During peak season, you may want to consider calling the campground before your arrival to see if they will hold a reservation for you.

Day Four: Free Day

- Set aside a recreational day for the beach and sports activities.
- Pick wild berries if they are in season and available near your campground.
- Lounge around the campsite while your children play.
- Attend nature shows and activities conducted by campground staff.
- Cycle or walk around the campground roads to see how the other campers are doing.
- Tidy up around your campsite, air out the sleeping bags, sweep out the tent and your vehicle.
- Drop off your garbage at the campground dump if you have not already done so.
- Purchase more firewood or ice if you are running low.

Day Five: Explore the Surrounding Region

- Refer to the information guide or campground brochures or talk to campground staff to determine what other attractions exist in the surrounding region.

Day Six: Cycling

- Refer to the information guide or brochures to determine what cycling options are available.
- If you plan to rent, get more information on where to rent bicycles for a day trip.

Day Seven: Fishing or Wildlife Viewing

- Talk to staff at the campground to determine where there is good fishing or wildlife viewing.

Day Eight: Free Day

- See **Day Four** or consider doing more of what you really enjoyed doing on one of the other days.
- If you enjoyed the campground and region, make notes on good campsites that you would like to stay at or other places in the region that you would like to return to in the future.
- If you are camping in the Ontario Parks system, ensure that you sample the ice cream available in the park stores or stores near the campgrounds. Many of these stores carry ice cream from the Kawartha Dairy Company. It is a tradition for us to have ice cream at least once on every camping trip, and the Kawartha Dairy Company supplies great ice cream to Ontario Parks.
- Start to clean up and pack some of your camping gear that you have finished using for this trip.

Day Nine: Departure

- Ensure that you start to break camp early so that you can vacate by checkout time.
- Remember to clean up your campsite, bag your garbage, and dispose of it.

CAMPING ACTIVITIES

Listed below are details on some of the more popular camping activities:

Beach and Swimming

You need to watch your young children at all times while at the beach. Some campgrounds are well suited for young children, having beaches that gradually slope into deep water. I have camped at other campgrounds where the beach sloped into deep water after fifteen to twenty feet. This can be dangerous for younger children. Most of the campgrounds that I camp at do not have lifeguards supervising the beach.

Safe Beach: Mew Lake, Algonquin Provincial Park

Shorelines may have rocky areas that require close supervision to ensure that children do not get injured.

Rocky Shoreline, Killbear Provincial Park

Ensure that your children are protected from the sun with adequate clothing and sun block.

Protection from the Sun

Ontario has hundreds of great beaches for swimming. Refer back to the "Trip Planning" chapter for some suggestions on Ontario Parks campgrounds that have great beaches.

Campfires

The most important concern when making a campfire is that the fire is contained and that no one gets burned. Young children need to be watched diligently to ensure that they do not play near the fire. Only start a fire in the designated fire-pit on your campsite and only if there is no fire ban in place.

A fire-pit will usually have stones around the perimeter and perhaps a metal cage on top. If you do not have a fire-pit on your campsite, then fires are probably not permitted. The campground office will advise you if campfires are permitted.

Campfire: Mew Lake, Algonquin Provincial Park

Most campgrounds that permit fires offer firewood for sale, either at the campground office or near the campground. Firewood is also usually available for sale privately near campgrounds. A bundle of wood sells for about $6 in Ontario. Depending on the size of the tree that the wood is cut from, it can be sold split into pieces that are one half, one quarter, or the full circumference of the original trunk or branch of the tree. You need to split this wood into smaller pieces and wood chips in order to start and maintain the fire. An alternative is to purchase kindling (starter) wood for approximately $3. Kindling wood is already cut into small pieces to start the fire. A bundle of wood usually lasts us two to four hours if we make a medium-sized fire, which provides enough heat to warm us up. Kindling wood is sold in much smaller bundles.

What You Need to Start the Fire

- **Dried wood**: Purchase one bundle of wood and see how your camping trip goes. Some campers burn a bundle or more a night, while others burn less. Purchase some kindling wood if you are having trouble starting the fire.

- **Axe**: This will help you to chop the precut firewood into smaller pieces that will ignite more easily.
- **Butane lighter or waterproof matches**: Use these to start the fire.
- **Kindling**: Use small pieces of birch bark, pine needles, moss, pencil-thin branches, dry wood chips that you chop, or paper that is dry and will easily ignite the fire.
- **Saw**: Most campgrounds supply precut firewood, so a saw is not necessary at those campgrounds. If the campground wood has not been precut or if you are backcountry camping, then pack a saw with you in order to cut the wood down to twelve-inch lengths that will fit into the fire-pit.
- **Poking stick**: Poking sticks can be used to control the fire. Wood can be repositioned so that it burns more easily. Any sturdy long stick will do.
- **Other accessories**: Folding lawn chairs with built-in coffee cup holders are mandatory for comfort and enjoyment these days. Some campers pack their own grill and throw it on top of the campsite fire-pit grill to cook on.

What You Need to Remember When Making a Campfire

- An adult should be supervising the campfire at all times.
- Watch your children carefully, as sometimes they may run around the campfire and throw things into the campfire or poke at it with a stick.
- Do not leave lighters or matches lying around where children can find them.
- Ensure that your camping gear and vehicle are away from the fire.
- Never build up the campfire so big that it is out of control.
- Always have water ready in the event that you need to put the fire out.
- Always dowse the campfire before leaving the campsite or going to bed.
- Do not burn any toxic materials. All recycling materials, including plastics, metals, cardboard, and so on, should be bagged separately for disposal. All other garbage should be bagged and disposed of as well.

Firewood Preparation Tips

- When splitting firewood, prop the wood up on end to split it. If one hand is used to support the wood that is standing on end, always keep it away from the area of wood that will be cut with the axe. Consider using a long stick instead of your hand to support the wood that is standing on end, so that you can safely split the wood without cutting your hand.
- A wood-splitting wedge is nothing more than a second axe blade that you use to hammer into the wood with the axe. Since the wedge is positioned and supported with your hand, you can easily miss it and strike your hand with the axe. A better way to split wood is to use your axe as a wedge and then drive it through the wood with a second piece of heavy wood or log. Use the log as a hammer to hit the back end of the axe blade. This way, the hand holding the axe blade is away from harm.
- When cutting small pieces and wood chips, take your time to avoid injury.
- Split the wood into three to four different sized pieces:
- Very small pieces of wood splints and chips, which will be used to start the fire
- Medium-sized pieces of split wood to build up the fire
- Larger-sized pieces of split wood to maintain the fire
- I usually split about half the bundle of wood into different sizes described above. The other half can be split later or tossed onto the fire as is, once the fire is strong.

Split Firewood

Fire-Starting Tips

Starting a fire under wet weather conditions can be challenging. The wood and bottom of the fire-pit will be wet, which will hinder your ability to start the fire. In addition, the paper that you use to start the fire may be damp and not ignite. Fires can also be difficult to start if there is too much wood or smoke in the fire-pit and a lack of oxygen to maintain the fire. Try these suggestions the next time you struggle with your fire:

- Place some of the starter firewood or wood that you have cut into fine chips on the ground in the fire-pit to provide a barrier from the damp ground below the fire. Cover a small area of the fire-pit ground and allow small gaps between the wood chips for ventilation.

Starting a Fire 1

- Place some dry crumpled paper, birch bark, or pine needles on top of the wood.
- Space dry thin pieces of wood on top in the form of a teepee-style tent. These pieces should be no more than one-half-inch thick.

Starting a Fire 2

- Light the paper, birch bark, or pine needles with your lighter or matches.

Starting a Fire 3

- As the fire starts to burn and gets bigger, gently add more small pieces of wood. Do not add too much wood at once, as the fire could be doused by lack of oxygen or by the moisture in the wet wood.
- Continue to add more wood as the fire gets bigger and stronger. Once the fire is burning well, throw in a large piece of split wood or log every now and then to maintain it.

Safety Tips

- Never let small children use the axe or saw.
- Always supervise older children who are using the axe or saw.
- Ensure that you store the axe and saw in a safe place that is out of reach from young children, such as the trunk of your vehicle.
- Do not throw flammable liquids onto the fire to start it. This is asking for trouble because the flames can spread dangerously in seconds.

What You Should Know: Campfires

- **Campfire bans**: Campfire bans are often imposed during periods when the weather is extremely dry and there is a threat of forest fires. The campground office will advise you if there is a ban when you arrive at the campground.
- **Campfire restrictions**: Many campgrounds impose other restrictions, such as campfires may not exceed one metre in height or diameter. Ensure that you understand all of the rules and regulations regarding campfires at every campground you go to.
- **Firewood restrictions**: Many campgrounds only allow you to burn wood that you purchase at or near the campground during your current trip. This means that you cannot bring firewood from home or from other campgrounds. Firewood that is transported to different regions across the province can spread diseases or insects.
- **No scavenging**: In most campgrounds, you are not permitted to cut trees or scavenge for fallen wood in the nearby forests. Be aware of any restrictions, so that you do not get fined. Fallen trees and branches are necessary to replenish nutrients in the ground, which allows the forest to continue to grow.

CAMP TRIPPER SECRETS: CAMPFIRES

- **Keep your firewood dry**: Always keep your firewood dry to ensure that it will burn easily. We store our firewood inside a green garbage bag, which we seal to keep the moisture out. The green garbage bag is then placed in our screen house or under a tarp for added protection from the rain.
- **Purchase firewood one bundle at a time**: I have seen many campers purchase bundles of wood that they were unable to burn because there was a lot of rain or they overestimated how much firewood they needed. After their camping trip was over, they would leave the wood at the campsite, and other campers would claim it in minutes. Wood is readily available and easily accessible at campgrounds. We purchase our firewood one bundle at a time, and sometimes a bundle lasts us several nights because of the following:
- Some nights, we are too tired to stay up for a campfire.
- Some nights are too hot and humid to enjoy a campfire.
- We may be at a friend's campsite.
- We may be enjoying other campground activities, such as the shows at the Ontario Parks amphitheatres.

Canoeing and Kayaking

Canoeing or kayaking has to be the ultimate experience when camping by lakes or rivers in Ontario. We have camped at many Ontario provincial parks that are equipped for canoeing and kayaking. Many campers bring their own canoe or kayak. We prefer to rent canoes and kayaks where we camp because it is much more convenient. Once our camping gear is loaded for a trip, we do not have the extra space for a canoe on the roof rack because our capsule is already there, loaded down with camping gear.

Canoes or kayaks that you rent come equipped with paddles, life jackets, pail, rope, and a whistle. You can research online using the Web links listed in the "Trip Planning" chapter to look up specific Ontario parks to check if they rent canoes and kayaks. If not available directly at the campground, there are usually outfitters who drop the equipment off for you and pick it up when you are done. In recent years, we have paid approximately $50 to rent large seventeen-footers for twenty-four hours, which is a very reasonable price. The seventeen-footers can comfortably seat two adults, two children, and gear for a day trip. Most parks that have backcountry canoeing or kayaking also offer maps. Always have a map to help you chart your direction and monitor your progress.

Canoeing: Lake of Two Rivers, Algonquin Provincial Park

What You Need for a Day Trip

- Canoe, paddles, life jackets, bailer, rope, and whistle: This should be provided with canoe rentals.
- Proper footwear: Sandals, Crocs, or sneakers in the summer; hiking shoes or boots are the best for cooler months or when you will be carrying the canoe and gear on portages.
- Layers of clothing: Layer your clothing to regulate body temperature, with more layers during the colder months of the year. Jeans and tops that are made out of cotton are difficult to dry when wet, so choose other fabrics. Consider the following:
- Windproof jacket or coat
- Fleece or wool sweater
- Shorts or pants
- Hat
- Thermal underwear, gloves, and warm hat during the colder months
- Water and food: The quantity should be appropriate for the trip. If the trip is four hours or more, pack a lunch; otherwise, snacks will do for shorter trips:

- Water bottle: At least one full bottle per person
- Suggested food: fruit, vegetables, sandwiches, crackers, granola bars, and nut mix
- Small first aid kit.
- Map and compass or GPS.
- Toilet paper.
- Sunscreen.
- Sunglasses.
- Bug repellant.
- Camera.
- Whistles: To signal others if you are lost.

Safety Tips

- Avoid canoeing alone.
- If canoeing and camping in the backcountry, let the park staff know your route.
- Ask the park staff about animals in the area and know what to do if you encounter them.
- Watch young children closely to ensure that they do not tip the canoe. Sometimes, they lean over the edge or engage in rough play, which could easily tip the canoe. We have instructed Jacob and Aaron to always sit in the middle of the canoe to maintain balance.
- Do not take any children canoeing who are too young to wear a life jacket or have inadequate swimming experience.

Strategies for Renting Canoes

- **Lightweight canoe**: A lightweight canoe is essential if you will do any portaging on your trip. Ask for a lightweight canoe, as it will save you the aggravation and frustration of struggling with one of those heavier monstrosities. We rent Kevlar canoes whenever they are available. You will pay a little more but it is worth every penny.
- **Canoe length**: If you only have two people, fourteen- or fifteen-footers will do. If you are canoeing with a family of four, request seventeen-footers.
- **Paddles**: If you are renting one canoe for your family, ask for two adult-sized paddles as well as a smaller one for your children to share when they have their turn at paddling. Always rent three paddles per canoe, in case one paddle breaks on the canoe trip.

Suggestions for Day Trips

There are many great lakes and rivers to canoe or kayak on in Ontario. Renting a canoe at one of the Ontario Parks campgrounds will give you the opportunity to explore the waterways. Here are some suggestions for family day trips:

- **Algonquin Provincial Park**: Canoes are available for rent and delivery at many lakes, including Canoe, Cannisbay, Mew, Two Rivers, Pog, Rock, and Opeongo. Canoe and Opeongo have outfitter stores onsite, and these lakes connect to many other lakes for backcountry trips. A return trip on Canoe Lake can be paddled in three to four hours. From Canoe Lake, another choice is to paddle to Bonita Lake, Tea Lake, and Smoke Lake for a day trip. If you rent at Two Rivers, you can canoe to the southeast end of the lake and continue to Pog Lake. If you paddle to the southwest end of Two Rivers, you can access the Madawaska River, which leads to some beautiful waterfalls where hikers swim in the summer. If you rent a canoe at Rock Lake, you can circle the lake in three to four hours, and this will allow time to see the cliffs. Another option is to head south from Rock to Pen Lake. Opeongo is a large lake and should only be paddled by experienced canoeists.
- **Grundy Lake Provincial Park:** You can canoe on several connecting lakes in the park, including Grundy, Gurd, and Gut. All lakes have beautiful views and offer excellent opportunities for swimming. The lakes are small enough to do a return trip in a day.
- **Killarney Provincial Park:** The lakes in Killarney are among the most beautiful in the province. Although most of the canoeing is more remote and will appeal to backcountry campers, it is possible to do a day trip to see some of the park. The main campground is located at George Lake, and a canoe trip around George Lake is well worth the time. If you have more time available, other beautiful lakes to explore include Killarney, O.S.A., and Norway, which are all accessible from George Lake.

Camp Tripper Secrets: Canoeing

- **Ensure that you canoe safely**: Statistics indicate that most canoeists who drown are young to middle-aged males who were not very skilled at canoeing, were not wearing life jackets, and were poor swimmers.
- **Avoid mishaps**: Paddle near the shoreline if you are worried about your family tipping the canoe, and instruct everyone to sit in the middle of the canoe at all times. Keep your footing and weight in the middle when stepping in or out of the canoe. Children will be tempted to lean over the side of the canoe and drag their hands in the water to cool them or grab water lilies and other floating vegetation and debris. Instruct them not to do this, as this can make the canoe tipsy.
- **Best paddling conditions**: Ontario lakes and rivers tend to be the calmest in the early morning or early evening.
- **Three seats**: Rent canoes with three seats if you have three paddlers. This way, everyone can paddle in comfort. Canoes with three seats are available at most Ontario Parks where I have camped.
- **Map**: Always take a map, as it will allow you to plan your trip, track your progress, and estimate your return time. If navigating with a compass or GPS, ensure that you know how to use it.
- **Trail markers**: Most backcountry canoe regions have trail markers at the designated portaging points between lakes. Always look for trail markers to help you pinpoint where you need to carry the canoe and gear. The trail markers should tie into the portaging points that are identified on your map. If no markers can be found, then pick landmarks such as inlets or islands along the lake or river that you can easily spot on your map. This will help you to chart your whereabouts on the map.
- **Word of mouth**: Talk to others you meet along the route, as they can usually provide you with significant information on where to see beautiful views, good places to stop for lunch, or whether they encountered difficult or swampy canoeing conditions. They may even be able to help you if you are lost.

Cycling

Cycling has become very popular at campgrounds in recent years, and bicycle rentals are available everywhere.

Cycling: Balsam Lake Provincial Park

What You Need for a Day Trip

- Bikes, helmets, and pant clips
- Bike repair kit: Tools, patches, glue, spare tube, and air pump

See "Canoeing and Kayaking: What You Need for a Day Trip" in this chapter for other essential gear

Consider Installing a Bike Rack

I have installed a bike rack over the back wheel of my bike. I have also installed a metal basket on top of the bike rack. The metal basket is extremely handy on cycling trips around the campground. You can use the basket for storing a knapsack containing your lunch, water bottle, bike repair kit, and other items listed above. This makes the ride much more comfortable. You will sweat quite rapidly if you have a knapsack strapped to your back while you cycle. If there is a store within riding distance of your campsite, you can also use the basket to transport supplies, including milk, bread, ice, and the newspaper.

Safety Tips

- Avoid cycling alone.
- Do not take young children on rugged mountain biking trails that are intended for older children and adults. Flat trails or

campground roads are the best for riding with young children. Ask park staff if their bike trails are rated for beginner, intermediate, or skilled riders.

- Check with the park staff before cycling on backcountry trails to see if any sections of the trails are in bad shape. For example, there could be flooding, fallen trees, or ice. If this is the case, you may need to pick a different trail to ride on.
- Ensure that all helmets are securely fastened.
- If you have a child seat mounted on your bike, check to ensure that it is fastened securely.
- Watch your young children closely, especially if they are riding on campground roads.
- Always have a map for long trails and trails that have a lot of connecting routes.

Suggestions for Day Trips

Here are suggestions for family day trips on safe trails in the Ontario Parks system:

- **Old Railway Bike Trail, Algonquin Provincial Park**: The Old Railway Bike Trail is relatively flat, as it runs along an old railway bed. The trail goes from Mew Lake Campground to Rock Lake Campground and is ten kilometres long (one way). You can also cycle directly to this trail from the campgrounds located at Lake of Two Rivers, Pog Lake, Kearney Lake, and Whitefish Lake.
- **Killbear Provincial Park**: Killbear has a six-kilometre (one way) trail that follows the main park road from the park entrance to Lighthouse Point Campground. The bike trail is accessible from all campgrounds in the park and is flat with some small hills along the route.
- **MacGregor Point Provincial Park**: There are four trails that collectively stretch about fourteen kilometres (one way) through the park. The trails are relatively flat throughout.
- **Rondeau Provincial Park**: There are three biking trails that provide twenty-three kilometres (one way) of good cycling through Rondeau's old roadways, marshes, oak forests, the Rondeau peninsula, and the Lake Erie shoreline.
- **Pinery Bike Trail, The Pinery**: The Pinery Bike trail stretches ten kilometres (one way) from the park store and follows the Old Ausable Channel. The trail is flat throughout.

Some campgrounds do not have dedicated bike trails; however, they may be situated near bike trails in the surrounding region. For example, if you are camping at Craig Leith Provincial Park, you can access a thirty-two-kilometre-long (one way) bike trail that links Collingwood to Meaford.

Fishing

If you are planning on fishing at parks or campgrounds where fishing is permitted, then you must have a valid fishing license and must know the fishing regulations for the area before you start fishing. Fishing regulations include the time of year when fishing is permitted, daily catch limits, and possession limits. Some parks will not permit live baitfish in their lakes. Other regulations may include no fishing near dams, how to dispose of live bait, and restrictions on boats with motors. Many parks and campgrounds will also be able to provide you with information on the fish stock in their lakes. For more information, call the park directly or check with the Ontario Ministry of Natural Resources.

Groceries and Shopping

Whenever possible, it is always a great strategy to buy groceries and go shopping on rainy or cold days, so that you can avoid the bad weather and pass the time doing something enjoyable. Check your cooler, food box, and other supplies before going shopping and make a list of everything that you need.

Hiking

Hiking on backcountry trails is an amazing way for you and your family to bond together, enjoy the outdoors, and explore the region where you are camping. Most Ontario parks, conservation areas, and national parks have hiking trails to explore.

Most parks that have backcountry hiking trails offer trail maps and leaflets that guide you and highlight the significance of the area where you are hiking, the distance of the hike, and estimated time to complete it. Leaflets are usually available at the starting point of the trail, and maps can be purchased at campground stores. For day hikes, the leaflets will do the job. For overnight hikes, you should purchase a map, which provides a more detailed illustration of the region. The maps and leaflets are great because they help you to monitor your progress through the trails and estimate how much farther you need to hike before you have completed the trails. Many of the backcountry maps for hikers and canoeists provide detailed trip planning information for the region,

Hiking: Centennial Ridges Trail, Algonquin Provincial Park

including camping gear, clothing, meal options, hiking or canoeing tips, and what to see. The maps may provide other information, including what to do if you encounter bad weather, get lost, are injured, or encounter bears. Just by packing the backcountry map, you have access to most of the information that you need for planning and carrying out your trip in the backcountry.

What You Need for a Day Trip

- **Proper footwear**: Hiking shoes or boots with support are the best for hikes. Purchase the lightest comfortable pair that you can find. Choose a size that allows you to add two pairs of socks for comfort and warmth. Polypropylene works well as the inner sock, and heavier wool works great as the outer sock. If you don't want to hike with a double layer of socks, then pack a second pair in case you wear through the ones you are hiking with. Try to avoid hiking with white cotton sport socks. I have been guilty of this. My feet were cold and uncomfortable when these socks got wet; polypropylene and other fabrics work better when wet.

Hiking Boots: Webster's Falls/Spencer Gorge Conservation Area

- Hiking trail leaflet, which is normally available at the foot of the trail in many of Ontario's provincial parks.
- Very young children - Child carrying sack, bottle, diapers, wipes, and baby food.
- See "Canoeing and Kayaking: What You Need for a Day Trip" in this chapter.

Safety Tips

- Avoid hiking alone.
- If hiking and camping in a remote area, let the park staff know your hiking route.
- Ask park staff about animals in the area and know what to do if you encounter them. For example, black bears are generally harmless as long as you do not threaten, startle, or feed them.
- Ask park staff if any sections of the hiking trail are not usable. For example, there could be flooding, fallen trees, or ice.
- Watch your young children closely to ensure that they do not trip and fall over roots and rocks.
- If you plan to use a child-carrying sack, ensure that it is in good condition before you start the hike.
- Give each of your children a whistle and advise them to use it immediately if they ever get lost, so that you can easily locate them.

Suggestions for Day Trips

Here are suggestions for family day trips on hiking trails in the Ontario Parks system:

- **Algonquin Provincial Park**: There are numerous trails along Highway 60, which is the main road that crosses through the south side of Algonquin Provincial Park. The trails are suitable for beginner, intermediate, and advanced hikers, and range in length from 0.8 to 88 kilometres. Trails that offer excellent panoramic views include Lookout Trail (1.9 km loop), Booth's Rock Trail (5.1 km loop) and Centennial Ridges (10 km loop). Other trails that are worth the visit include Spruce Bog Boardwalk (1.5 km loop), Peck Lake (1.9 km loop), and the Beaver Pond Trail (2.0 km loop).
- **Arrowhead Provincial Park**: The Big Bend Lookout, which is a short walk from the main campground road, offers a scenic view. The Stubb's Falls Trail (2 km loop) has a beautiful waterfall that flows under a bridge along the trail.
- **Bon Echo Provincial Park**: The Cliff Top Trail (2 km loop) offers a panoramic view of the region and Mazinaw Lake.
- **Grundy Lake Provincial Park**: The Gut Lake Trail (2.5 km loop) offers scenic views of the Canadian Shield and Gut Lake.

For those families with more experienced hikers and older children, some excellent backcountry trails include the following:

- **Algonquin Provincial Park**: The Highland Hiking Trail (35 km loop) provides an excellent view of Highway 60, Lake of Two Rivers, the airfield, and surrounding region. You can pick up the trail from the airfield, which is situated between the Lake of Two Rivers and Mew Lake campgrounds, and do a two- to three-hour return trip to see this section of the trail.
- **Killarney Provincial Park**: The La Cloche Silhouette Trail (100 km loop) is long, but it offers some spectacular hilltop views. There are shortcuts that you can take to see the best parts of the trail. For example, if you are backcountry camping at Norway Lake, you can do a ten-hour loop (approximately 20 km) to hike to Silver Peak and the surrounding region. Silver Peak is the third highest mountain in Ontario at 539 metres.

- **Lake Superior Provincial Park**: The Coastal Trail (63 km one way) has magnificent views of the Lake Superior shoreline. You can select a section of the trail near the main campground to hike for a day trip.

WHAT YOU SHOULD KNOW: HIKING

- **Trail layout**: Most trails are "loops," meaning that the trail follows a circular route that ends where it starts. The total trail length for loops is equal to the total length of the hike. If a trail isn't a loop, then the hiking distance indicated will most likely be for hiking one way from your starting point to the other end of the trail. For one-way trails, you need to double the distance to include your return trip. Be aware of this, as it will have a huge impact on your hiking trip if you are not prepared for it. Always know where the hike will take you and how long it should take before starting the hike.

CAMP TRIPPER SECRETS: HIKING

- Leave early so that you won't hit the crowds on the trails.

Rush Hour on the Hiking Trails: Lookout Trail, Algonquin Provincial Park

- **Trail map**: Always take a trail map, if available. This will allow you to plan your hike, provision for it, track your progress, and estimate your return time. I have never had a compass or a GPS and have never been lost on any hiking trip because I always follow the trail maps and trail markers on the trails. If you are using a compass or GPS, ensure that you know how to use it before starting your hike.
- **Trail markers**: Most hiking trails have trail markers, which are little coloured plastic or metal pieces that are nailed onto trees. Always look for trail markers on your hike, as it is confirmation that you are still on the trail and have not gotten lost. If you are hiking on a trail and the trail markers disappear, backtrack immediately until you find the last trail marker. Then, look closely for the next trail marker and continue following the trail. Some trails have more prominent trail markers, such as numbered posts.

Trail Post: Bat Lake Trail, Algonquin Provincial Park

- **Word of mouth**: Talk to other hikers that you meet along the trail. They may be able to help you confirm your whereabouts on the trail, help you if you are in trouble, or provide you with updated trail information.

- **Hiking stick**: Consider using a hiking stick. I use one on rugged trails to maintain my balance, and it has saved me from getting bad sprains on numerous occasions when I lost my footing.

Organized Activities

If there is a campground information guide or brochure available where you go camping, it will most likely list organized activities that are available for you to participate in. Organized activities with park staff can include group hikes, children's activities, special events in the park, and evening shows and talks. Most Ontario provincial parks and conservation areas offer activities. Check with the park staff for more details. We always take advantage of the organized children's activities when available. It is a great opportunity for children to learn about the environment where they are camping or hiking, including plants and wildlife.

Picking Wild Berries

Depending on the region of Ontario where you are camping, you may have the opportunity to spend an afternoon picking wild berries to eat. In the Canadian Shield, north of Toronto, there are many campgrounds that have wild blueberries and raspberries, which are in season in late July through August. You can find out more by asking campground staff if there are wild berries in the area when the berries are usually in season. For picking wild berries, consider the following:

- Wear pants and long sleeve shirts with a hat (the bugs may be a nuisance).
- Keep insect repellant and sunscreen off your hands while picking berries.
- Bring a Tupperware-style container or pot to store your picked berries in.
- Bring a full water bottle for each picker.
- Wait for drier, windier conditions, as there will be fewer bugs to contend with.

Last summer on a trip to Algonquin Provincial Park, we picked so many wild blueberries and raspberries that we did not need to purchase any fruit during the camping trip. The wild berries are excellent on top of your cereal first thing in the morning. Some people take the berries home and make jam with them.

Sports and Recreation

Many campgrounds in Ontario have recreation fields with baseball diamonds. Some campgrounds do not have recreation fields, but have a large open space by the beach. Other campgrounds have playgrounds for smaller children. Jacob and Aaron have found that it is easier to make friends at campgrounds when they take advantage of these facilities.

Playground: Long Point Provincial Park

Surrounding Region

If you tour the surrounding region of your campground, you can easily find plenty of things to do. For example, explore villages, towns, and stores; see art and nature exhibits, museums, local crafts, and environmental features; go to amusement parks, movies, or theatres; and so on.

We usually reserve these activities for rainy days because a lot of time is spent driving in the car and visiting the surrounding region. If you do not know what is available, go to the local tourist office or chamber of commerce, and you should be able get everything you need. This may also be a good time to fill up the gas tank and do some grocery shopping.

Walks: Campground

When you just arrive at your campground, a great activity is to explore the campground on foot and see how all of your neighbours are enjoying their camping trips. Enjoy the walk, but please ensure that everyone in your family knows how to find their way back to the campsite. More campers probably lose their way back to the campsite from the washroom than get lost on hiking trails. We make it a practice to memorize our campsite number when we arrive at the campground. In addition, we sometimes walk as a family, with the campground map, to ensure that we know our way around the campground. You will need to walk to the washroom quite frequently, so ensure that you know your way. A good practice is to write down your campsite number on separate pieces of paper and give one to all members of your family who are old enough to walk on their own.

Wildlife Viewing

It is very difficult to plan to see wildlife in its natural habitat. It just happens when it happens. A few years ago, we were camping in Algonquin Provincial Park when a moose ran by our campsite around lunchtime. It was not the typical place or time of day to see a moose, but we had one of our closest views of a moose. After the moose left, we followed his tracks along the campground road but then lost the trail when he went back into the forest. Another time, while backcountry camping at Killarney Provincial Park, I woke up at 6:30 one morning to find three moose in our campsite. They quickly fled as soon as they heard me unzip the tent. If you want to spend a day viewing wildlife, here are some of the tricks that we have learned:

- **Dawn and dusk**: The early hours in the morning after daybreak and the evening before dark tend to be the best times to see birds and mammals. It is well known that moose like to lick the salt that gets thrown on the roads to melt winter ice. The ice melts and washes the salt into the roadside ditches. The moose can be spotted along roadsides in the early mornings and evenings in May and June in some parts of Ontario. On one camping trip, I counted twelve moose, just by driving up and down Highway 60 in Algonquin Provincial Park for about one half hour in the morning and one half hour in the evening. Remember to drive slowly and be alert so that you do not accidentally collide with a moose. If you see wildlife while driving, always pull off to the shoulder and stop, so that you do not create a dangerous situation for other drivers on the road. Another great way to spot wildlife is by canoe at dawn and dusk.

Moose: Algonquin Provincial Park

- **Word of mouth**: Talk to others about places where they have seen wildlife. For example, the Mizzy Lake Trail in Algonquin Provincial Park is known to be a great trail to spot wildlife. Knowing this, I hiked the trail once and saw moose drinking water in a pond near the trail.
- **Low, flat, wet areas**: Areas that are low, flat, and wet are the best areas to spot wildlife, especially if there aren't a lot of tall trees. Areas with bogs, meadows, and ponds all come to mind.
- **Binoculars and camera**: Do not forget your binoculars and camera.

7 Keeping the Trip Memorable

Camping can be a lot of work and things can go wrong, so you need to know how to deal with problems and setbacks that arise during your trip. Here are the problems and setbacks that we have encountered along, with the strategies that we have used to overcome them to ensure that our family camping trips remained memorable:

CAMP TRIPPER SECRETS: MEMORABLE TRIPS

SETTING FAMILY RULES

It is important to have family rules on camping trips because the rules allow everyone to know what the baseline code of conduct is for all members of the family. If everyone follows the rules, there is less stress in the family, and the camping trip becomes more enjoyable. Consider having your family meet to jointly set the rules for everyone to follow on the camping trip. This will ensure that everyone respects the needs of the family and does his or her part to help facilitate a successful camping trip. Here are some of our family rules:

- **Clear the dining area after every meal**: Our policy is to clean up our dining area after every meal. This ensures that friendly visitors from the forest do not arrive unannounced to scavenge through our food box or cooler. All dishes and cutlery are washed, dried, and placed in the cutlery box. All food is placed back into the cooler or food box and returned to the vehicle, and the table is wiped down. Any trash is placed in garbage bags away from the dining area. If you consistently do this, you will have a clean campsite, and the raccoons and chipmunks will dine elsewhere.

- **Always tidy up**: We try to tidy up around the campsite whenever we are finished using camping gear. Any loose gear, toys, or sports equipment is packed when not being used: "Whoever uses it, puts it away when finished with it." This will ensure that your equipment does not get lost or water damaged from rain.
- **No shoes in the tent**: Every time you wear shoes in the tent, you track in dirt, sand, leaves, and mud. Your camping gear will quickly get soiled, and nobody likes to sleep in a dirty tent. What's more, the wear and tear of your shoes on the tent floor will contribute to a more rapid breakdown of your tent. Our policy is to take our shoes off before entering the tent. If it is raining when you enter the tent and there is no dry place to store the shoes outside of the tent, then by all means bring the shoes in, but have a spare garbage bag that you can lay them on to reduce the mess inside the tent. If the tent has an outside vestibule that is adequately sheltered from the rain, even better: keep your shoes there. When we camp in the summer, we switch to sandals before bedtime. This way, we can leave our sandals outside by the tent entrance. If the sandals get wet, it is not a huge problem because they dry quickly.
- **No wet clothes in the tent**: Most of us worry about rain seeping into our tents and drenching our sleeping bags. I am willing to bet that more of us have wet sleeping bags because we left wet swimsuits and towels on them. I have done this so many times over the years, when changing clothes after a swim. Once the sleeping bag is wet, it is uncomfortable to sleep in. Always hang wet clothing and towels on your clothesline.
- **Keep your clothes neat and tidy**: All clean clothing should remain properly folded and stored in clothing bags. This way, it remains clean and ready for use. All dirty clothing should be placed in the dirty laundry bag. There is nothing worse than seeing dirty socks and underwear lying on top of the sleeping bags and pillows.
- **Don't disturb others**: We all need quiet time and our own space. This means using quiet voices and no banging dishes or

opening the car doors late at night or early in the morning. If we are awake while others are sleeping, then we find quiet ways to amuse ourselves!

SPREAD THE LOAD

Camping is a lot of work. There is research, shopping, packing, driving, setting up camp, preparing meals, cleaning up, planning day trips, and other activities as well as breaking camp and unpacking at home. It is not fair for one person to be stuck with all of the work, because that person will soon tire of the lengthy list of responsibilities, become irritable, and feel resentful of the others.

In our family, we spread the load around so that everyone helps out with chores. As Jacob and Aaron get older, we empower them by giving them more and more responsibility. In the early years, they were responsible for tidying up their toys and making sure that they did not track dirt into the tent. As they got older, they started helping to set up the table for meals and to wash dishes afterward. Now they help out with packing their sports bags, loading the car, setting up camp, planning day trips, carrying their knapsacks for hikes, and breaking camp. This way, they help the family and appreciate the trip more. We as parents also have more time to enjoy the trip when everyone chips in with the chores.

Little Helper

COOKING

If you have just purchased a new camping stove, learn how to use it in your backyard at home before you leave on your camping trip to ensure that you know how to use it and that it works properly. Review the instructions and ask the sales staff at the store if you are still uncertain of how to properly operate it. Practice lighting your stove, adjusting the heat level, and turning it off outside in a ventilated area, away from anything that can catch fire. You should also test it out annually before going on your camping trips to ensure that it is still operational. Here are a few more points to remember when cooking with your stove:

- **Where to place your camping stove**: The camp stove should be placed at one end of the picnic table, with children and adults seated away from the stove for safety. The stove should also be placed far enough away from screen house walls, overhanging tarps, and any other camping gear, so that the flames from the stove do not burn it. The picnic table must be level in order for the stove to work properly. You can level the picnic table by inserting rocks and wood chunks under the legs.

Where to Place Your Camping Stove

- **Be careful when starting your stove**: This is the time when it can flame up and get dangerous. I once melted a hole through a screen house wall because the stove was too close to it and I opened the gas a little too much. When igniting the stove, use as little gas as possible.

- **Never leave the stove unattended by adults.**
- **More safety precautions**: Please read carefully:
- Reduce the heat or turn off the stove if it is flaming radically or looks very hot.
- Only use the recommended fuel and carry it in approved aluminum fuel canisters or the original can that it was purchased in.
- Do not attempt to refill the fuel tank when the stove is in use or is hot.
- Never use a stove inside your tent or any area with poor ventilation.

KITCHEN CHORES

There are other chores that need to be done to maintain a well-running kitchen while you are camping. Divide up the chores, and give everyone in your family some responsibility:

- **Obtaining campground water**: Someone in your family will need to be responsible for filling the water container at the campground water tap and carrying it back to the campsite for cooking, drinking, and washing dishes. If the campground only has cold water taps, then water will need to be boiled to wash the dishes. The best time to boil water is while you are eating your meals. This way, the water is hot as soon as you are finished eating.
- **Disposing of waste**: Always bag your trash daily for disposal at the campground dump to avoid animals rummaging through your garbage. Before washing your dishes, scrape all food from plates, pots, and pans into a garbage bag. Please note that recycling is in place at many campgrounds now. Ontario Parks campgrounds, such as Algonquin Provincial Park, now have "Moloks." Moloks are large recycling bins. Two thirds of the Molok is below ground level so that gravity can naturally compact the waste, and the cooler underground temperature helps to reduce odour. The Molok lids are bear-proof and are labeled to indicate what type of recycling waste goes in each bin.

- **Ice in your cooler**: Check the ice in your cooler and drain the excess water from melting ice daily. You need to replace the ice in your cooler every few days; otherwise, your food will spoil in no time. If any food smells or looks bad, then throw it out because it is not worth getting ill from eating spoiled food. Ensure that you know where the campground ice supply is located, and do not wait until the last minute to replace it (sometimes, the ice is sold out). Ice is normally available for sale at or near the campground. Always purchase an ice block instead of ice cubes when available. The ice block is more compact and stays frozen longer.
- **Keep your cooler in the shade**: Whenever possible, keep your cooler in a shady spot, away from the sun. When storing the cooler in the car, park the car in a shady spot whenever possible to keep the contents of your cooler cold longer.

STAYING DRY

I have been drenched many times on camping trips over the years. On Thanksgiving weekend, 1985, I was camping in Algonquin Provincial Park during a torrential downpour throughout the day and evening. We killed off part of the evening by driving to a restaurant in Whitney to watch the Toronto Blue Jays in the World Series. When we returned to the campsite, the bottom of the tent was drenched right through to the point that there were puddles inside the tent. Our campsite was too low, and water accumulated in puddles all around our tent and seeped in. The tent was so wet that we had to sleep in the car overnight and went home the next day to dry out.

In August 2004, we had heavy rain for twenty-four hours while camping at Bon Echo Provincial Park. We stayed relatively dry because we used tarps over our tent and dining area and were camped on higher ground. The people camping across from us put up a tarp over their fire-pit, so that they could keep their fire going during the rain. The strategy for keeping the fire going worked well; however, they didn't have a tarp over their tent and got drenched. They ended up going home the next day to dry out.

My most recent wet memory was camping in Balsam Lake Provincial Park in Ontario in May 2008. It rained for almost three days nonstop. It can be very discouraging when you are camping and it is constantly raining. Given enough rain, anyone's spirits can be dampened to the point where they want to pack up and head home early. Nobody likes camping in the rain; however, the more prepared you are, the more you will be able to make the most of your trip. Many of the following suggestions have already been mentioned in other sections of the book:

Coping with Rainfall

- **Tarps**: Always hang a tarp over your tent and dining area if you do not have a screen house.
- **Groundsheet**: Place a groundsheet inside your tent to provide a moisture barrier between you and the wet ground.
- **Sleeping gear**: Keep your sleeping bags, pillows, and blankets off the floor and away from the walls of the tent to avoid dampness. Place your sleeping bags, pillows, and blankets on top of air mattresses or sleeping pads, which can then be placed on top of the groundsheet inside the tent. Make it a habit to ensure that these items are completely on top of your air mattresses or sleeping pads when you are out of the tent during the day.
- **Footwear**: Always wear sandals or Crocs without socks during rainy summer days. Although your feet will be cold and wet, your socks and other shoes will be dry and ready for use when it stops raining. Your sandals and Crocs will dry out quickly. For cool, wet weather; wear rubber boots or hiking boots that have been treated to repel water.
- **Dress appropriately**: Wear rain gear and appropriate layers to accommodate for the temperature.
- **Select a campsite with partial sun**: A campsite that receives some sun will allow you to quickly dry out and warm up after heavy rainfall.
- **Stow gear when not in use**: Before going to sleep each night, store all camping gear safely away from any potential rainfall. We move our lawn chairs, sports equipment, and other gear into the screen house. We take all clothes and towels off the clothesline and drape them on the car seats to dry overnight. Finally, we throw a tarp over the bikes to reduce water damage. We also do this during the day if there is a chance of rainfall. I have seen many campers with drenched camping gear over the years because they failed to stow their camping gear before rainfall.

Morning Dew

Ontario has warm weather and high humidity, which causes morning dew. As your camping gear radiates heat during the night, it cools down and dew appears on the surface of the camping gear. If you do not want your gear to get wet, stow it.

Activities

Here are some suggestions for how to pass the time on those rainy camping days:

- **Indoor recreation**: Ensure that you pack board games, cards, kid's games, books, magazines, newspapers, and writing paper. Use this time for planning day trips and making adjustments to your agenda.
- **Visit the surrounding region**: This is a great time to make a list of what groceries you need, do some shopping, and see local towns, villages, and other attractions.
- **Search for great campsites**: If you enjoy the park that you are camping at, rainy days are excellent days to drive around to search for good campsites for return trips. Take a pen and paper and record the campsite numbers. Pay special attention to where the rain is collecting on the campsite on those rainy days. If you see large puddles of water on any campsites, do not record the campsite numbers, as you could end up getting drenched from the ground up if you camp there.
- **Search for other campgrounds**: In Ontario, a campsite permit that is valid in one provincial park will allow you entry to other provincial parks for the time period that the permit is valid. In essence, your permit can be used as a free day permit at other provincial parks. On rainy days, you can drive to other parks and scout them out to see if you want to book future camping trips there. In July 2007, we were camping at Silent Lake Provincial Park. One day we had heavy rainfall, so we toured the region and ended up staying at Lake St. Peter Provincial Park for a good part of the day. In between rain showers, we hiked, checked out campsites, and swam at the beach. We had free access to the park that day because we had a valid permit to Silent Lake Provincial Park.
- **Picnic shelters**: Some campgrounds have picnic areas with public picnic shelters. The shelters are a great place to meet other campers, learn about their camping experiences, and exchange notes on what to see in the region.
- **Do your laundry**: If you decide to do your laundry on a rainy day, go to the laundry facilities as early as possible, as many other campers will be doing the same thing.
- **Get extra sleep.**

SEVERE WEATHER

I have camped through many thunderstorms over the years, and the same question always comes up: What do you do when there is a bad thunderstorm with lightning, heavy winds, or hail? Do you stay in the tent, go to the car, or go somewhere else? Not being sure what to do, I've done all of them. You should always take appropriate shelter if the weather conditions look dangerous.

Rainbow After a Heavy Storm: Mew Lake, Algonquin Provincial Park

With lightning, you want to avoid high points (including tall trees or high ridges), metal, water, branches, and other debris that could fall and hit you. Consider the "30-30" Lightning Rule: When there is less than thirty seconds between the sound of thunder and the sight of lightning, you should find shelter. You should also wait in the sheltered area until thirty minutes past the last thunder. To find appropriate shelter, consider the following:

- Move to a comfort station or your hard-topped vehicle if you are in a tent or tent trailer. If you go to your hard-topped vehicle for protection, do not touch any metal parts inside the car if there is lightning.
- Move to a low-lying area, crouch down, cover your head, and avoid being near the tallest objects such as isolated trees if you

are not near a comfort station or hard-topped vehicle. Remove all metal objects and do not lie flat on the ground, as this will make you a larger target.

- If your tent is under trees that may fall on it, then wait outside in the storm in a spot that looks safe from falling branches.

You should also look for shelter immediately if there is large hail. If there is heavy rain or flash flooding, stay away from streams and rivers. If a twister or tornado hits, go to the campground comfort station. Strong winds may be capable of overturning your vehicle. You should always have access to a radio to listen to the local weather channel. Usually, you can get a heads-up warning two to six hours before a major storm strikes and possibly drive away before the storm hits. Weatheradio Canada is a nationwide network of radio stations broadcasting weather and environmental information twenty-four hours a day for this purpose. Tune in whenever you can to ensure that you are prepared for any storms. The best thing to do with severe weather is stay calm and go with your gut feeling, and usually you will do the right thing.

Pesky Bugs

I will never forget the time when, camping as a child in Algonquin Provincial Park, the black flies were so bad that we had bites all over our bodies. It was late June and it had been rainy and cool that month. I remember having red welts and itchy skin for days after returning home from the camping trip. In fact, my mother was bitten so badly that her eyes were swollen over to the point where she could not open them. We had to drive her to the hospital to get some medical attention.

Over the years, I have come to realize that sometimes you need to make adjustments to accommodate the things that you cannot change in your life. The same rule applies to camping in bug season. I have one of the less common blood types. I guess bugs find me more appealing, almost like dessert, because my blood tastes a little different. Anyway, my rule is to not go camping in black fly country during black fly season. For me, this means that I avoid my favourite camping spots in Ontario's Canadian Shield during late May and June. During black fly season, I camp at other regions in Ontario that are drier and warmer.

How do you know when it is bug season? It depends on the region that you are camping in, the climate, the time of year, and so on. After you go camping in your region for a few years, you quickly come to learn when the bugs are biting. If you are not certain of the bug season, I recommend calling the park office in advance and asking them when the bug season is typically at its worst there. Here are more suggestions:

- **Pack the best bug repellant that money can buy**: The oily bug repellants that you rub onto your body are more effective and last longer than the ones that you spray on. Apply the repellant liberally to all exposed flesh. Repellants that contain Deet are considered to be good, especially for protecting against West Nile virus. Apply the repellant to your hat and it will help to keep the pesky critters from landing on your head. Sprays work the best on hats and clothing. Incidentally, Deet should not be used on very young children. For young children, you also need to use milder repellants for comfort and to minimize the burning sensation if they accidentally rub it into their eyes.
- **Dress properly**: Wear clothes that cover your entire body:
- Long-sleeve shirts and long pants
- Socks and shoes, as exposed feet are a favourite for the bugs
- Hats, because bugs also love your head, especially when you start sweating on hikes
- Lighter colours, which seem to be less attractive to bugs than darker colours
- Screen netting over your face, if the bugs are really bad
- **Avoid certain scents:** Do not wear makeup, perfume, cologne, or scented deodorant, as these fragrances attract bugs.
- **Select an appropriate campsite**: Try to camp in more open areas where there is a breeze instead of near swamps, creeks, marshes, and bushes.
- **Keep your tent and screen house zipped shut at all times**: Bugs enter through any little gap they can find, as they are very opportunistic. Do not encourage them by leaving your tent and screen house unzipped. Turn off your flashlights at night when entering the tent and screen house, as light attracts bugs.

VISITORS FROM THE FOREST

Over the years, we have had chipmunks, squirrels, and raccoons visit our campsite for food on a few occasions. Each time, it was because we had left food unattended or did not properly clean up and put food away after eating. I was on a backpacking trip in the Grand Canyon many years ago. When leaving food unattended there, you had to properly hang it in packs, out of reach of animals. I can remember shining my flashlight into the sides of the canyon walls at night and seeing the eyes of ringtail cats in the dark.

Naturally, they were waiting for everyone to go to sleep, so that they could climb down from the canyon walls and search for a meal. These raccoons were extremely dexterous. Anyone who did not seal off the smell of food, zip up their packs, or hang their packs properly woke up to discover that the raccoons had ravaged their packs. Here are some suggestions to ensure that you do not have any uninvited visitors:

- **Do not leave exposed food unattended**: Do not leave exposed food unattended, and never eat or store food, soap, toothpaste, or anything else that has a fragrance in your tent.
- **Clean up immediately after every meal**: Clean up all food scraps and wipe up all food crumbs and grease immediately after every meal. Ensure that all tins, plastic, and other disposable containers used for food are rinsed and bagged immediately. Bag all organic waste in sealed bags and dispose of it in the dumpster daily.
- **Food storage bin**: Use a large plastic storage bin, as already suggested, to store all dry and canned food on car camping trips. Any food that is not in your cooler should be stored in this bin. These containers are weatherproof and seal out the scent of food reasonably well. Store these containers along with your cooler in your vehicle when not in use.
- **Tupperware and ziplock bags**: Use Tupperware or ziplock bags to store unwrapped food products.
- **Keep cooler and food bin shut tightly when not in use**: This reduces the smell of food.
- **Do not feed wild animals**: In Ontario, it is against the law to feed wild animals, and you can be fined for doing so. Feeding wild animals causes them to lose their fear of humans, and this can create dangerous situations.

Black Bears

Back in August 2005, we were on a camping trip at Killbear Provincial Park. One morning, I was the first one in our family to wake up, around 6:30 AM. As I unzipped our tent and looked across the road to the campsite facing us, I saw a black bear rummaging through their camping gear in the screen house. As soon as the bear saw me, he ran away. The people who were camping there had left some food in their dining area overnight, which drew the attention of the wandering bear. As soon as these campers woke up, I told them that a bear had visited their campsite. They had a look of terror on their faces. Always put your food away and clean up when you have finished eating.

I am a firm believer that bears are generally timid and will run away from you at first sight, provided that you have not fed, startled, or angered them. In all my years of camping, this is the only time that I stumbled upon a bear, and he ran away from me at first sight. When camping in Ontario, always read the information guides provided to learn about the animal situation at the park and follow what is recommended. I read the information guides all of the time, just so I know what to do if I have a bear encounter. Here is the most common advice that I see in the information guides:

- Do not feed or approach bears.
- In most cases, a bear will flee when it hears or smells you, long before you even see it.
- If you are near a building or vehicle, then go there for safety.
- If the bear charges you, it is usually a bluff, so waive your hands and start talking to him so that you appear bigger than you are to him and slowly back away from the area. Bears have bad eyesight, and this may be enough to scare him away. If you are with others, stay as a group, but make sure that the bear has a clear escape route.
- Use a whistle, air horn, or bear spray if you have them. You could also try banging pots together or using bear clappers. I have also read articles about people scaring off bears with bright flashlights.
- Do not turn and run, as this may trigger a predatory response in the bear.
- Do not climb a tree, as bears are excellent climbers.
- Fight back as hard as you can with black bears using stones, sticks, and your fists if you have to.

If you are camping in polar bear country in northern Ontario or other provinces, then you should review the strategies for bear encounters with parks staff there. The same applies if you are camping where there are grizzly bears.

POISON IVY

Poison ivy is a plant that you do not want to go near on any camping trip. If you are not sure what poison ivy looks like, each stem has three leaves. The centre leaf tends to have a longer stalk than the two leaves on the sides. There could also be small clusters of whitish-green flowers, which appear in June or early July, and white berries grow in mid-July. Poison ivy patches are usually ankle high; however, they can grow higher. Poison ivy can grow in many places: along the edges of meadows, in open forests, along riverbanks or roadsides, and near beaches. Provincial parks staff usually control poison ivy near the edges of trails and high-use areas of campsites. Beyond that, you should be careful where you walk.

SLEEPING WELL

Sleeping well when you are camping is extremely important. Otherwise, how can you be rested enough to participate in various activities? Not only am I a light sleeper who can be woken up by the slightest noise, but I also have difficulty sleeping when I am cold. Here are some suggestions for sleeping well:

Sleeping in Cold Weather

- **Cold nights**: If you or anyone in your family is having trouble sleeping because of cold nights, then refer back to the "Car Camping Startup Costs: Sleep" section of this book. In addition, consider the following strategies that we deployed on a recent camping trip to Point Farms Provincial Park, where the temperature fell to 0°C at night:
- If you are using an air mattress, place a foam mat on top of it to insulate you from the cold.

Foam Mat on Top of Air Mattress

- If you have any old sleeping bags, use them as blankets to throw on top of your new sleeping bags on the cold nights. We have zipped together one side of two sleeping bags to create a giant quilt, which is large enough to cover four sleeping bags.
- **Wear a hat and socks**: Since we lose most of our body heat through our head and feet, try wearing a wool hat and socks to bed.
- **Don't wear too many layers**: You should only have one layer on your body: pajamas, a wool hat, and socks. If you wear more layers, then you will sweat and impede your body's ability to heat up the sleeping bag.

Light Sleepers

If you are a light sleeper, then you can lose a few nights of sleeping while camping. Why? You could be woken up by the sound of rain splattering on your tent, strong winds, birds chirping in the early morning, cars traveling on nearby roads, or noisy campers who do not respect quiet time during the night. As a light sleeper, here is what I have done over the years to help ensure that I get a good night's sleep on my camping trips:

- **Select an ideal campsite**:
- Select a campsite that is on less heavily traveled campsite roads and away from the main highway that connects to the campground.
- Pay extra for a premium campsite that is larger or spaced farther apart from other campsites.
- Do not select a campsite that is located beside toilets, showers, and other busy areas.
- Book a "radio-free" campsite (if available at your campground), as excessive noise is not permitted at these campsites.
- **Pack earplugs**: Earplugs can eliminate about 80 percent of the noise that will keep you awake at night. When I have my earplugs on, I barely hear the rain, wind, birds, cars, or people.
- **Stay away from campsites with electrical hookups**: If you are camping with a tent, do not select a campsite in the section of the campground that has electrical hookups. The noise from neighbouring campers with air conditioners or heaters running all night may keep you up.
- **Noisy neighbours**: If asking noisy neighbours to keep the noise down does not work, check at the campground office to

see what other options are available. Usually there is a local number to call for the park warden or police. This is the best solution for avoiding a confrontation with noisy neighbours. Over the years, on several occasions I have seen the police make noisy campers leave their campsites.

BEING A GREAT NEIGHBOUR

Here are several suggestions to ensure that you have a great time with all of your neighbouring campers:

- **Campground rules**: The campground rules are for the safety and enjoyment of all campers and are usually posted at the campground office, so please follow the rules.
- **Do not walk through occupied campsites**: Other campers have rented campsites for the time that they are there. Please show respect and walk along the campground roads and trails without taking shortcuts through occupied campsites.
- **Do not be excessively noisy**: All campgrounds have quiet times during the night when excessive noise is not permitted. However, respect for your fellow campers should be extended into the day as well. Don't be excessively loud when camping.
- **Do not hog the facilities**: The showers, sinks, and toilets are to be shared by all campers. Always show consideration for others when using the facilities. Also, the facilities should be left with the same level of cleanliness that you found them in: "leave no trace."
- **Washing dishes**: Wash your dishes at your campsite or the designated dish washing stations, whichever applies at your campground. Do not wash your dishes at the water supply taps or in the washrooms. Campground staff and other campers frown upon this.
- **No speeding in the campground**: Children will be playing on the campground roads. Drive slowly, so that you do not accidentally hit someone or create unnecessary dust in the campground.
- **Supervise your children and pets**: You are responsible for monitoring your children and pets. Ensure that they do not disturb other campers or get hurt.
- **Don't litter.**

BEING A GREAT BACKCOUNTRY VISITOR

Here is how you can do your part to keep the backcountry clean and safe during your canoeing, kayaking, cycling, fishing, and hiking trips:

- **Do not litter the lakes, rivers, and trails**: Anything that you pack in needs to be packed out or properly burned in a backcountry fire-pit.
- **Help those in trouble**: Always help those in trouble on the lakes, rivers, and trails, however you can.

CAMPING WITH FRIENDS

We often go camping with other family and friends on camping trips. Here are some suggestions to ensure that you can get campsites that are close to each other at the campground:

- **Make reservations in advance**: Refer back to the "Trip Planning" chapter. Discuss the campgrounds and campsites with your extended family and friends and make the reservations as early as possible.
- **No reservations**: If you and your friends do not have a campsite reservation and plan on securing campsites when you arrive at your target campground, then plan to arrive at the campground together to increase your chances of securing campsites that are near each other. If you arrive first and your friends are arriving later in the day, you can post your name and campsite number on the campground office bulletin board for your friends to see when they arrive. Another option is to communicate with your friends by cell phone. Cell phone service is available at many campgrounds that are located near towns and major highways. Please note that most campgrounds frown upon excessive use of cell phones!

Most campgrounds have a restriction of how many people can camp on any particular campsite. In the parks where we camp, the limit is six people per site. The exception to this rule is families that are larger than six people (e.g., two parents and five children). If you have four people in your family and your brother and his wife are planning on joining you on a camping trip, they may be able to camp at your campsite as well. Your family of four plus he and his wife equal six people. This meets the people restrictions per site. You also need to check that the site is large enough to accommodate the extra tent and if the extra vehicle can be parked at the campsite or a designated parking area nearby. Campsite restrictions are usually posted on the campground Web site, or you can ask at the park office when you arrive.

THEFT

In all my years of camping, I have never had anything stolen while on a camping trip; I guess campers are honest people. Here are a few precautionary measures you can take to ensure that you go home with all of the camping gear that you brought on your trip:

- **Out of sight on your campsite**: Never leave anything of value lying around the campsite, in the tent, or in the screen house. I have never left my wallet, camera, or anything else of value unattended at the campsite. Always lock up good quality bikes, when not in use. If you have your own canoes or kayaks, then pull them well into your campsite where they are not as easily accessible.
- **Out of sight in your vehicle**: When storing valuables in your vehicle, ensure that they cannot be viewed through the window and lock your vehicle. Always store anything of value in a locked trunk, in the glove compartment, or under a blanket or other cover if you have a minivan or station wagon. It is well known that thieves will smash windows and remove items from unattended vehicles left along roads near hiking trails and canoe routes.

EXTENDING YOUR STAY

Oftentimes, you will find that you are enjoying yourself so much at a campground that you wish to extend your stay there. Extending your stay at a campground has become increasingly difficult since the evolution of online reservations on the Internet. The more popular campgrounds can have campsites reserved beyond your departure date, making it difficult for you to stay at your campsite or switch to a vacant campsite. Consider the following strategies to extend your stay at a campground:

- Check with the office as soon as possible to determine if your campsite is available beyond your departure date, so that you can extend your stay. If your campsite has been reserved for your departure date, ask campground staff if other campsites are available and book one that meets your needs. From my experience, you will have to be very lucky to extend your stay on the same campsite during the summer months.

- If you have a few days left before your booked departure date, check with the office daily to find out about recent campsite booking cancellations. Walk or drive around the campground and look for sites where people appear to be packing up to go home. If you find such campsites, check the departure dates on their permits, which are usually inserted in the campsite posts. If they are leaving days before their booked departure dates, then the chances of their campsites being available to you are very good. Make a note of the campsite numbers and ask about availability at the office.

DÉJÀ VU

Each year, we decide which campgrounds we want to return to. I highly recommend that if you have a favourite campground, you return there as often as possible. Returning to our favourite campgrounds allows us to reconnect with our past as a family and to enjoy the present time. We usually book one week at our favourite campground and two to three weeks at new campgrounds, in order to broaden our camping experience. During your camping trips, you will come across campgrounds that you enjoy and plan to return to one day. If you have found such campgrounds, here is what you can do:

- **Campsites:** Always have a pencil and paper handy to record the numbers of your choice campsites where you would like to stay if you return in the future, as mentioned earlier in this book. I have seen many campers stay at the same campsites, during the same weeks, year after year. Oftentimes, we will talk with them and say, "Hey, I remember you being on the same campsite at the same time last year."
- **Trails and canoe routes:** Over time, if you do a lot of hiking, biking, and canoeing the way we do, the trails and routes can blur together in your memory. Make notes of the great trails and canoe routes that you complete, in case you choose to revisit them in the future.

8 Breaking Camp

When the camping trip is over and it is time to pack up and go home, the goal is to pack all camping gear clean and dry at the campsite. All sand, dirt, stones, sticks, and other debris must be removed, and everything must be dry to avoid mold, mildew, and equipment breaking down before it is time. If your camping gear is wet or dirty when you pack it, you must dry it out and clean it up as soon as possible after returning home. If you can remember this rule, you should get many years of enjoyment out of your camping gear.

PACKING STRATEGY

In the "Keeping the Trip Memorable" chapter, we said that everyone should help to tidy up and "whoever uses it, puts it away when finished with it." Following this strategy, a lot of your camping gear should already be bagged and stowed away in your vehicle or other sheltered area on the campsite. If you have followed the strategy of putting all dirty clothing in a laundry bag, as mentioned in the "Setting Up Camp" chapter, then all of your dirty clothes will be segregated and bagged. Taking small steps like these cuts down on the amount of work involved when you break camp.

When you start packing, always wipe off and dry out whatever you can first, since drying time can be anywhere from a few minutes to several hours depending on how wet your camping gear is and how sunny and warm the weather is. Here is our breaking camp strategy:

1. **Remove Contents from Tent**
- Remove all sleeping bags from the tent, unzip them, and drape them over the clothesline to dry them out.

- Shake the sand and any other debris out of the sleeping bags at the same time.
- Repeat this process for your air mattresses, sleeping pads, and ground sheet.
- Remove all remaining gear from inside your tent and pack it in your vehicle.

2. **Packing the Tent**
- Once the tent is empty, sweep out the inside with a small brush or whisk and scoop up the dirt with a dustpan. Then wipe up any excess moisture with rags or paper towels.
- Remove the fly from the outside of the tent and drape it over the clothesline to dry it out. Shake it well to remove the excess moisture and debris. Flip it over every now and then to quickly dry it out.
- Give the tent a good shake to remove any excess moisture, and let it dry with the framing poles and stakes still in place.
- After the tent is dry to touch on the surface, remove the tent stakes and poles and let the tent collapse to the ground. Be careful when folding up the poles. Keep your fingers clear of the joints that fold over. I have gotten many bruises and cuts over the years, jamming my fingers between the poles.
- Tap the tent poles and stakes gently against a hard surface to force out any dirt and sand that is trapped. Then, let the poles and stakes dry out.
- Flip the tent over to allow the bottom side to dry out. The bottom side of the tent will usually have the most moisture build-up and take the longest to dry.
- Once the tent, fly, poles, and stakes are dry, shake them again to remove any remaining dirt and pack them tightly in the tent stuff sack and put it in your vehicle.

3. **Remove Contents from Screen House**
- After you have finished cooking, turn off all switches on your stove and let it cool down. Ensure that the fuel tank lid is shut tight. When the stove is cool, wipe off all grease and dirt.
- Ensure that all food is put away and all dishes and cutlery have been washed and dried.
- Clean out and wipe off your cooler, dry food box, and cutlery box.
- Drain out excess water from the melting ice in the cooler.

- Dispose of any food that you do not plan to bring home.
- Pack the cooler and boxes into your vehicle.
- If you have a vinyl tablecloth, wipe it clean and pack it.
- Remove any other gear from the screen house, including the picnic table.

4. **Packing the Screen House**
- Give the screen house a good shake to remove any excess moisture and let it dry with the framing poles and stakes still in place.
- After the screen house is dry to touch on the surface, remove the stakes and poles and let the screen house collapse to the ground.
- Tap the screen house poles and stakes gently against a hard surface to force out any dirt and sand that is trapped.
- Let the poles and stakes dry out.
- Flip over the screen house to allow the inside to dry out.
- Once the screen house, fly, poles, and stakes are dry, shake them again to remove any remaining dirt and pack them tightly in the stuff sack and put it in your vehicle.

5. **Packing Tarps**
- If you hung any tarps for your camping trip, shake them out well while they are still hung.
- Gently pull down on one end to allow any trapped rainwater to easily drain off the top of the tarp.
- Remove the ropes from the tarp and the trees.
- If the ropes are wet, dry them out; otherwise, roll them up and put them in your vehicle.
- Lay the tarps flat on the ground to dry.
- Shake the tarps and flip them over every now and then to speed up the drying process.
- Once dry, brush off any debris, fold them up, and put them in your vehicle.

6. **Pack Everything Else**
- Lawn chairs, hammocks, and any other gear that you have needs to be packed into your vehicle.
- If you brought a canoe or kayak, fasten it to the top of your vehicle.
- If you brought bikes, load them onto your vehicle.

7. **Dowse the Campfire**
- Pour any excess water from your washing basin or cooler into the fire-pit to dowse the campfire.
- You are responsible for making sure that your fire is out before you leave the campsite.

8. **Bag All Trash**
- All trash needs to be bagged and disposed of at the campground dump.
- Ensure that you do not leave your trash in the fire-pit or anywhere on your campsite; otherwise, you may be fined.
- Campers go by the "leave no trace" motto, meaning "leave the campsite clean."

9. **Final Campsite Check**
- After all of your camping gear has been packed in your vehicle, take a final walk around the campsite. Check everywhere on the campsite that your family has been during the course of your camping trip. Believe me, you will find Frisbees, soccer balls, and badminton birdies scattered across the campsite and surrounding shrubs. I have a bad habit of forgetting to take down my clothesline. Check your campsite thoroughly before departure, as this is probably the most likely way that camping gear gets lost.

Start packing up as early as possible on departure day. It can take anywhere from one to three hours to break camp. You also need to vacate your campsite by the time specified at the campground, which could be anywhere from 11:00 AM to 2:00 PM. If it is raining on your departure day, then you have my sympathy, because everything can get wet, and you will have to dry it out at home. Packing wet when going home is one of the biggest disappointments when you go camping; however, nothing is perfect in life.

Going Home

What You Should Know:
Going Home Early

If you plan on cutting your trip short, many campgrounds will offer a partial refund, provided that you notify them in advance. Check with the campground office to see if they give partial refunds.

Camp Tripper Secrets:
Shorten Your Packing Time

- **Pack nonessential camping gear the day before departure**: Make it a habit to dry out, wipe off, and pack any nonessential camping gear the day before your departure. Here is some of the camping gear that we usually pack the day before:
- **Recreation gear**: Beach toys, life jackets, and hammocks.
- **Screen house and tarps**: Only pack them if you are fairly certain that it will not rain overnight or if you are planning on leaving first thing in the morning.

- **Tidy up the day before departure**: Clean out your tent, dining area, cooler, stove, dry food box, dish and cutlery box, stove, and vehicle, and dispose of all garbage. Also check around your campsite to make sure that you have collected all of your loose camping gear.
- **Campsite with partial sun**: If you have a campsite with partial sun, look for a sunny spot on your campsite and drag your camping gear there to dry it quickly on departure day.
- **Empower your children**: Take the time to train your kids to help out with breaking camp. Initially, it will take you longer, but over time you will pack much more quickly as you give your kids more and more responsibility. Jacob and Aaron help with packing all camping gear. The more responsibility you give them, the happier they become!

9 Maintenance of Your Camping Gear

You must take steps to maintain your camping gear to ensure that it is operational for many years. Here are some suggestions:

STORAGE

After your camping trip is over, ensure that all of your gear is clean and dry before you stow it away. Do not stow your camping gear in any place where there is moisture or freezing temperatures. A tent that gets wet in a leaky garage will break down in no time from mold and mildew. Some materials break down when exposed to freezing temperatures, even if it is dry. Air mattresses and self-inflating sleeping pads have parts that are glued together. Freezing and thawing temperatures can break the seal over time, allowing air to escape when inflated. Consider storing your sleeping pads and air mattresses indoors. With self-inflating sleeping pads, it is recommended that you do not roll them up for storage. Instead, you can store them unraveled, under your bed at home.

With some of the higher end sleeping bags, the manufacturer may recommend that the sleeping bags be stored in larger sacks that are provided free of charge or available for sale at the retail outlet. The larger storage sack allows room for the sleeping bag to expand and helps to reduce the wear and tear on the sleeping bag, which can occur when it is tightly compressed. With these sleeping bags, the smaller stuff sacks should only be used for your camping trips. If you have one of these sleeping bags, store it indoors in the larger sack, or store it unrolled, perhaps under your bed.

Try to keep your sleeping bags as clean as possible during your camping trips because this will minimize how often you need to wash the bags. When you wash your sleeping bags, use a front load machine with cold water, a gentle wash cycle, and mild liquid detergent. The top load machines are much harsher on the sleeping bags and can damage them more easily. Only wash the sleeping bags when absolutely necessary, as excessive washing will cause wear and tear. If using a dryer, use low heat to avoid damage to the sleeping bag.

REPAIR OR REPLACE DEFECTIVE GEAR

Check over your camping gear annually. The best time to do this is before your camping season starts. Allow yourself enough time before your first camping trip to repair or replace any defective gear.

Tents and Screen Houses

In all my years of camping, I have owned many different tents and screen houses. Now that I do mostly family car camping, I have found that my tents and screen houses need to be replaced every two to three years (this is assuming that I camp for three to four weeks per year with a family of four). Here is what we have learned from our camping experience:

Zippers

It is usually a zipper that breaks first on tents and screen houses. When I say zipper, I mean the main zipper that is used to enter and exit the tent or screen house. This problem has occurred with our last three tents and screen houses. Why? Many reasons:

- Zippers nowadays are not as durable as the older and larger metal zippers.
- Zippers are often accompanied by a fabric that drapes over the zipper to keep the rain off. This fabric can easily get caught in the zipper, which puts stress on the zipper, thereby causing it to prematurely break. Always use two hands—one hand on the zipper and the other on the fabric—when zipping and unzipping.
- Children sometimes struggle with the zippers, which causes additional wear and tear.

A broken main zipper on the tent presents a grave problem if rainfall or bugs are expected. If the zipper breaks, the problem will require immediate attention. The first time a zipper broke on our family tent, we had one of the older tents with a heavy metal zipper; a few of the teeth fell out of the zipper, making it inoperable. As we had about five nights remaining on that trip and the tent was already about six years old and out of warranty, we promptly drove to the nearest town and purchased a replacement tent that came with a lightweight main zipper. The main zipper on the new tent broke within one year on another camping trip. As it broke on the second-to-the-last day of our camping trip, we draped a tarp over the tent and secured it to keep bugs and rain out for the night. Once the camping trip was over, we returned the tent to the store where we purchased it, as it was still under warranty. The store did not give us a replacement tent. Instead, they shipped the tent out to the manufacturer for repair, and we did not get the tent back for several weeks. Most warranties on tents nowadays are with the store where it was purchased for seven to fourteen days; you send the tent back to the manufacturer after that. In fact, some stores request that you deal directly with the manufacturer after you purchase the tent.

The point that I am making here is that if your tent breaks during your camping trip, you have to decide if you want to purchase a replacement tent immediately at the nearest town or return home early from the trip and have the manufacturer repair or replace your tent. You should consider this when purchasing a tent. Some people do not believe in buying the best quality tents because even though these tents may come with extended warranties, they are not prepared to go home early from a camping trip because of a broken tent and wait several weeks for it to be repaired or replaced.

Framing Poles

The hollow steel poles that accompany many screen houses nowadays are the worst poles. They are bulky and heavy, and they easily rust and buckle. We had such a pole rust and buckle on us during a camping trip. To extend the life of the screen house, I used a small car radiator hose clamp and fastened it around the rusty spot that buckled. This allowed us to continue using the screen house for the rest of the camping season that year.

The fiberglass poles with bungee cords or shock-corded poles that accompany most tents and screen houses nowadays are better because they are quite durable, light, and compact. Over time, I have found that they can crack. If the crack is major, the pole will have to be replaced by taking it back to the manufacturer. If the crack is minor, duct tape applied over the crack several times may temporarily repair the damage. Aluminum poles are lightweight, durable, and the best. However, aluminum poles are very expensive. If you have extra money to spend on camping gear, purchasing a tent or screen house with aluminum poles is a good investment.

Fabric

I have found that the tent and screen house fabric is most susceptible to damage when setting up or breaking camp. Specifically, the sleeves in the fabric where the poles get inserted can rip. You can avoid such damage by taking extra care when inserting or removing the poles from the sleeves when you set up and take down your tent and screen house. Once it rips, you need to stitch it together immediately with very strong thread to avoid further damage.

Leaks

If it rains long enough or hard enough, water can penetrate your tent or screen house. The water usually leaks in through the stitching in the fabric. When you purchase your tent or screen house, check to see if the manufacturer has sealed the seams. There should be a clear shiny strip that is applied on the seams. If the seams have not been sealed, you can apply a sealer to all stitching to waterproof it. Over time, the sealer wears off and you need to reapply the sealer on the seams as leaks are found. Purchase a bottle of seam sealer from a store that sells camping equipment. Set up your tent in your backyard on a dry, sunny day. Shake the bottle and apply it on all seams on the outside and inside of the tent while the tent is standing. After a few hours, the seam sealer will have dried and you can take down and pack your tent. Remember that the most important areas to seal are those that get direct exposure to water, including the seams on the fly and those along the bottom sides of the tent where the fly does not cover.

Screen houses that are made out of polyethylene (tarp material) can easily be patched with duct tape if they leak. For the duct tape to be more effective, patch the hole on both sides of the fabric so that the two pieces of duct tape can seal together where the hole is. If your screen house is leaking along the seams, then apply the seam sealer product to it.

Tip: As mentioned in previous chapters, a properly placed tarp will almost guarantee that you will not get wet inside your tent or screen house, even if the seams on your tent or your screen house are not properly sealed.

Sleeping Pads and Air Mattresses

Self-inflating sleeping pads and air mattresses lose air over time. Usually, it is the seams in the self-inflating sleeping pads and mattresses that weaken and allow the air to escape. When this happens, there is not much you can do except refill with air as needed. When it gets to the point where I have to add air every night, I replace the pad or mattress with a new one. With a new air mattress, I usually do not have to add air a second time in the course of a week. You can add years of life to your self-inflating sleeping pads and air mattresses by storing them indoors where the temperature does not drop below zero, so that the seams do not weaken with freezing and thawing. Storing self-inflating sleeping pads and air mattresses unraveled is also a good idea because it reduces the amount of stress on the seams.

Tarps

Tarps are extremely durable and should last you for many years. With age and use, your tarps may eventually develop small tears and holes. Examine your tarps and repair any holes and rips as soon as possible to avoid the problem from getting worse. Again, using duct tape, patch both sides of the tarp to ensure that the duct tape is securely fastened. When I purchase a new tarp, I unravel it at home and check it over for holes and rips immediately. Secondly, I check that none of the grommets are defective.

WHAT TO SALVAGE

When your camping gear has reached the end of its useful life, you should always check to see what you could salvage for use on future camping trips. Here are some suggestions:

- **Stakes**: Keep the tent and screen house stakes. Stakes often get lost or broken at campsites, and you will need extras. Newer stakes also tend to not be as robust as the older ones. If you have older, stronger stakes, keep them for future use. In most cases, stakes can be used on any tent or screen house and do not need to be specifically designed for specific equipment.
- **Guy-ropes**: Anchoring ropes can easily be lost, so keep the old ones.

In Closing

Camping is a lot of work, and not everyone is up to the challenge or has the desire or level of interest to participate in a camping trip. It took me many years of camping with family and friends to realize this. Between planning, organizing, packing, setting up, maintaining, and taking down camp, you will be busy, but in between there will be plenty of time to enjoy your trip if you have prepared for it. As the saying goes, "Nothing that is worth doing comes easy," and this applies to camping. If you are up to the challenge and have the passion for it, in my opinion, camping is the greatest way to get away from it all. After all, what better way is there to get in touch with nature? I have enjoyed camping all of my life and would not trade a night in my tent under the stars for any five-star hotel room.

Yes, there will be cold nights when it is hard to get to sleep or those rainy days when you are stuck in the tent or screen house, under a tarp, or in the car trying to stay dry. There will also be those days when you wish that time would stand still … when you get up in the morning, watch the fog move across a lake, see the sunrise, listen to sound of a loon's call, hear the fluttering wings of a heron in flight over a lake, spot a deer on the horizon, go for an adventurous hike in the woods, canoe through the backcountry, or go biking and discover things that you have never seen before. And of course, there is the campfire and sleeping under the stars at night. This is why I believe what I say: there is no experience like camping.

I am fortunate in that everyone in my family enjoys camping. Although we each have varying interests, there is enough common ground between us that we can adapt to address the needs and desires of everyone, which maximizes the chances of a successful and memorable camping trip. For the most part, we all enjoy adventure, hiking, canoeing, swimming, campfires, and sleeping outdoors. We also all hate the rain and the bugs. This works well for us and is critical to ensuring the success of a camping trip. We focus on doing the activities that everyone likes and deal with the rain and bugs collectively when we have to. If you have never gone camping before, then consider taking your first trip with someone who has camped before, so he or she can show you the basics and so you can get a taste of what camping is all about.

I have met a few people who view camping as being an activity for less educated, lower income people who cannot afford to stay at a hotel or purchase a cottage. This is rubbish and a dreadful pity; this lack of understanding prevents many people from exploring and experiencing the world in a way that they can never see it. Having been brought up in a family that started camping and then had a cottage for many years, I had the privilege of experiencing both worlds. While staying at the family cottage, I always had my best moments emulating camping activity, unbeknownst to me. This included taking the canoe for a paddle around the lake, hiking through the rural countryside, or having a campfire at night. Camping allows me to fulfill my passion for adventure, which I cannot achieve by going to the same cottage every weekend. I wish you many happy years of successful and memorable family camping trips!

Index

Y

Z